The Spirit of Hope

Byung-Chul Han

The Spirit of Hope

With illustrations by Anselm Kiefer

Translated by Daniel Steuer

polity

Originally published in German as *Der Geist der Hoffnung: Wider die Gesellschaft der Angst* © Byung-Chul Han, 2023

This English translation © Polity Press, 2024

Polity Press
65 Bridge Street
Cambridge CB2 1UR, UK

Polity Press
111 River Street
Hoboken, NJ 07030, USA

ISBN-13: 978–1-5095–6519–1 – hardback

A catalogue record for this book is available from the British Library.

Library of Congress Control Number: 2024936390

Typeset in 11pt on 15pt Janson Text
by Cheshire Typesetting Ltd, Cuddington, Cheshire
Printed in Canada by Marquis Book Printing

The publisher has used its best endeavours to ensure that the URLs for external websites referred to in this book are correct and active at the time of going to press. However, the publisher has no responsibility for the websites and can make no guarantee that a site will remain live or that the content is or will remain appropriate.

Every effort has been made to trace all copyright holders, but if any have been overlooked the publisher will be pleased to include any necessary credits in any subsequent reprint or edition.

For further information on Polity, visit our website:
politybooks.com

CONTENTS

List of Illustrations

Hope is a spring, it is the leaping of a gulf.
(Gabriel Marcel, *Being and Having*,
Westminster: Dacre Press, 1949, p. 79)

Prelude

A spectre is haunting us: it is fear. We are constantly confronted with apocalyptic scenarios: pandemics, world war, the climate catastrophe. Images of the end of the world or the end of human civilization are conjured up with ever greater urgency. In 2023, the so-called Doomsday Clock stood at ninety seconds to midnight, apparently the closest the dial has ever been to the end of the final hour.

Versions of the apocalypse abound. They are even offered as commodities: *apocalypses sell*. An apocalyptic mood is spreading, not only in real life but in literature and film as well. In *The Silence*, Don DeLillo describes a total technological blackout. Surface temperatures and sea levels are rising in literature, too. *Climate fiction* has become a new literary genre. T. C. Boyle's *A Friend of the Earth*, for instance, tells the story of an apocalyptic climate change.

We are facing multiple crises. Anxiously, we confront a bleak future. There is no hope. We muddle through from crisis to crisis, from one catastrophe to another, from one problem to the next. Amid problem-solving and crisis management, life withers. It becomes *survival*. The breathless *survival society* is like a terminal patient trying everything to find a cure. But only hope can give us back that *life* that is more than mere *survival*. It is hope that opens up a *meaningful horizon* that reinvigorates and inspires life. Hope presents us with a *future*.

The climate of fear precludes hope. With fear, depression takes hold. Fear and resentment drive people into the arms of the right-wing populists. They breed hate. Solidarity, friendliness and empathy are eroded. Growing fear and resentment make society more brutal, and ultimately threaten democracy. In his farewell address upon leaving office, US president Barack Obama rightly said, 'Democracy can buckle when we give in to fear.'[1] Fear and democracy are incompatible. Democracy flourishes only in an atmosphere of reconciliation and dialogue. Those who believe that their opinions are unimpeachable and who stop *listening* to others cannot be citizens.

Fear is a popular tool for rulers. It makes people obedient and susceptible to blackmail. In a climate of fear, people worry about repression and so do not dare voice their opinions freely. Hate speech and shitstorms also create fear and thus hinder the free expression of opinions. We even *fear thinking*. We seem to have lost the *courage to think*. Thinking proper provides access to what is altogether other. A climate of fear produces a continuation of the *same*. Conformism spreads. Fear blocks the paths towards the other. What is other escapes the logic of efficiency and productivity, which is a *logic of the same*.

The rule of fear makes freedom impossible. Fear and freedom are mutually exclusive. Fear can turn society itself into a prison, create a kind of quarantine. Fear puts up warning signs. Hope, by contrast, sets up signposts and pathmarks. Only when there is hope can we be *on our way*. Hope provides *meaning and orientation*. Fear, by contrast, stops us in our *tracks*.

We fear not just viruses and wars. People are also preoccupied with 'climate fear'. Climate activists openly admit that they are 'afraid of the future'. Fear deprives them of their *future*. We cannot deny that 'climate fear' is justified, but the pervasive *climate of fear* is a cause for concern. Our problem is not a fear of pandemics but a *pandemic of fear*. Acting out of fear is not *a way of acting that supports a sustainable future*, which would require a *meaningful horizon* and action that forms *part of a narrative*. Hope is *eloquent*. It *narrates*. Fear, by contrast, is *incapable of speech, incapable of narration*.

The German 'Angst' (middle high German 'angest'; old high German 'angust') originally meant 'narrowness'. Angst suffocates any feeling of vastness, of perspective, by narrowing down and blocking our view. Someone who is fearful feels cornered. Fear is accompanied by a feeling of being caught and imprisoned. When we are fearful, the world seems to be a prison. All the doors that lead out into the open are locked. Fear blocks off the future by closing our access to what is *possible*, what is *new*.

Hope is fear's opposite in a linguistic sense, too. The entry on 'hoffen' [to hope] in Friedrich Kluge's etymological dictionary says: 'by leaning forward, one tries to look further, with greater precision'.[2] The hunting term 'verhoffen' still carries the old meaning of 'hoffen': 'to stand still in order to listen, to hearken, to pick up the scent'. Thus, it is also said 'Der Rehbock verhofft' [The roebuck stops short]. Someone who hopes tries to pick up the scent, that is, tries *to find the right way to go.*

Only in the deepest despair does true hope arise. The deeper the despair, the more intense the hope. It is no accident that *Elpis* (the Greek goddess of hope) is represented as the child of *Nyx*, the goddess of the night. Among *Nyx*'s siblings are not just *Tartarus* and *Erebus* (darkness), but *Eros*. *Elpis* and *Eros* are related. Hope is a dialectical figure. The negativity of despair is constitutive for hope. Saint Paul also emphasizes the negativity inherent in hope: 'we glory in tribulations also: knowing that tribulation worketh patience; And patience, experience; and experience, hope: And hope maketh not ashamed.'[3]

Despair and hope relate to each other like valley and mountain. The *negativity* of despair is inscribed in hope. Nietzsche spells out their dialectical relationship as follows:

> Hope is the rainbow over the cascading torrent of life, swallowed up a hundred times by the foam and forming ever anew, crossing the torrent with tender and graceful audacity where its roar is the wildest and most dangerous.[4]

There could be no better description of hope. It possesses a 'tender, graceful audacity'. Those who act with hope act audaciously and are not distracted by the rapidity

4

and toughness of life. However, there is also something *contemplative* about hope. It *leans forward and listens attentively*. The receptivity of hope makes it *tender*, lends it *beauty* and *grace*.

Hopeful thinking is not optimistic thinking. Unlike hope, optimism lacks *negativity*. It knows neither doubt nor despair. Its essence is *sheer positivity*. Optimism is convinced that things will take a turn for the good. For optimists, the nature of time is *closure*. They do not know the future as an open space of possibility. Nothing *occurs*. Nothing surprises. The future appears available. The real future, however, is characterized by *unavailability*. Optimists never look into an unavailable *distance*. They do not reckon with the unexpected or incalculable.

Optimism does not lack anything. It is not *on its way*. But hope is a *searching movement*. It is an attempt to find a firm footing and a sense of direction. By going beyond the events of the past, beyond what already exists, it also enters into the *unknown*, goes down *untrodden paths*, and ventures into the *open*, into *what-is-not-yet*. It is headed for what is still *unborn*. It sets off towards the *new*, the *altogether other*, the *unprecedented*.

Optimism requires no effort. It is something given, taken for granted, like someone's height or other of their unaltering characteristics. As an optimist, 'you are chained to your cheerfulness like a slave to his oar, a glum enough prospect'.[5] An optimist does not need to provide reasons for adopting his attitude. The existence of hope, by contrast, cannot simply be taken for granted. It *awakens*. Frequently, it must be *called upon, appealed to*. Unlike optimism, which lacks all determination, active

5

hope is characterized by *commitment*. An optimist does not properly *act*. Action is always associated with risk, and an optimist does not take risks.

There is no fundamental difference between optimism and pessimism. One mirrors the other. For the pessimist, time is also *closed*. Pessimists are locked in '*time as a prison*'.[6] Pessimists simply reject everything, without striving for *renewal* or being open towards *possible worlds*. They are just as stubborn as optimists. Optimists and pessimists are both *blind to the possible*. They cannot conceive of an *event* that would constitute a surprising twist to the way things are going. They lack *imagination of the new* and *passion for the unprecedented*. Those who hope put their trust in possibilities that point beyond the 'badly existing'.[7] Hope enables us *to break out of closed time as a prison*.

Hope also needs to be distinguished from 'positive thinking' and 'positive psychology'. In turning away from the *psychology of suffering*, positive psychology aims to engage exclusively with well-being and happiness. Negative thoughts are to be immediately replaced with positive ones. The aim of positive psychology is to increase happiness. All negative aspects of life are ignored. It imagines the world as one giant department store, where whatever we want we can buy.

According to positive psychology, everyone is responsible for their own happiness. Its cult of positivity means that the afflicted have only themselves, rather than society, to blame. Positive psychology suppresses the fact that suffering is always *socially mediated*. It psychologizes and privatizes suffering. What really causes suffering – the social context of delusion – is left untouched.

The cult of positivity isolates people, makes them egotistic, and reduces empathy. People are no longer interested in the suffering of others. Everyone looks only to their own happiness and well-being. In the neoliberal regime, the cult of positivity dissolves societal solidarity. Unlike positive thinking, hope does not turn away from the negative aspects of life. It remains *mindful* of them. Hope does not isolate people; it unites and reconciles them. *The subject of hope is a We.*

The Epistle to the Romans states that 'hope that is seen is not hope: for what a man seeth, why doth he yet hope for?'[8] The temporal mode of hope is *not-yet*. Hope opens itself up to the *coming*, for *what-is-not-yet*. It is a spiritual attitude, a spiritual *mood*, that elevates us above what is already there, above what is already present. Hope, according to Gabriel Marcel, 'is engaged in the weaving of experience now in process, or in other words in an adventure now going forward'.[9] To hope means 'to put one's trust in reality', to believe in it so that it carries with it a future. When we hope, we become *creditors to the future*. Fear, by contrast, deprives us of all belief, withdraws all credit granted to reality. It thus prevents the future.

Following Derrida, we may distinguish between two forms of future, namely 'future' and 'l'avenir':[10] 'The future is that which – tomorrow, later, next century – will be.' This future is 'predictable, programmed, scheduled, foreseeable'. It can therefore be administered. The future as 'l'avenir', by contrast, concerns *events* that occur altogether unexpectedly. It escapes all calculation and planning. It opens up an unavailable *space of possibility*. It announces the unforeseeable *coming of the other*. 'L'avenir' is characterized by its unavailability.

7

Experiences such as deep happiness or passionate love have their *negative pole*, which is the ground in which they set down roots and flourish. There is no elevation without depth. Love, too, is *passion*. Simone Weil affords suffering the status of a condition for the possibility of love: 'I felt only in the midst of my suffering the presence of love, like that which one can read in the smile of a beloved face.'[11] Without negativity, intensity is impossible. The sprawling and omnipresent 'Like', today's withered form of experience, lacks all negativity. 'Like' is the fundamental formula of consumption. Negativity and intensity evade consumption. Hope also has intensity. It represents a deep *prayer of the soul*, a *passion* that awakens in the face of despair's negativity.

Being a *passion*, hope is not passive. Rather, it has its own kind of determination. It seems to resemble the brave *mole of history* who confidently digs tunnels endlessly through the darkness. In his *Lectures on the History of Philosophy*, Hegel compares spirit to such a mole wearing seven league boots:

> Spirit alone is an onward striding. Spirit often seems to have forgotten and lost itself, but inwardly ... it is ... ever forward (as when Hamlet says of the ghost of his father, 'Well said, old mole! Canst work i' the earth so fast?'), until grown strong in itself it bursts asunder the crust of earth which divided it from the sun, its Notion, so that the earth crumbles away. At such time, when spirit has put on the seven league boots, the encircling crust [the world that was], like a soulless decaying tenement, crumbles away and spirit displays itself arrayed in new youth.[12]

The spirit of hope is likewise an *onward striding*. It *keeps working away* amid darkness. There is no light without darkness.

The current omnipresent fear is not really the effect of an ongoing catastrophe. We are plagued by vague fears that have structural causes and therefore cannot be linked back to concrete events. The neoliberal regime is a *regime of fear*. It isolates people by making them *entrepreneurs of themselves*. Total competition and the increasing pressure to perform erode society. This narcissistic isolation creates loneliness and fear. Our relation to ourselves is also increasingly dominated by fear: fear of failing; fear of not living up to one's own expectations; fear of not keeping up with the rest, or fear of being left behind. The ubiquity of fear is good for productivity.

To be free means to be free of compulsion. In the neoliberal regime, however, freedom produces compulsion. These forms of compulsion are not external; they come from within. The compulsion to perform and the compulsion to optimize oneself are compulsions of freedom. Freedom and compulsion become one. We voluntarily submit ourselves to the compulsion to be creative, efficient, authentic.

The often-invoked concept of creativity, in particular, prevents the emergence of *something radically different*, *something unheard of*. Creativity is associated with a new form of production. The society that promotes creativity, the performance society, is a service society. It is the successor to the disciplinary society, which belonged to the era of industrialization. Creativity establishes itself as a neoliberal dispositif that, like any dispositif, has a compulsive character. Its purpose is solely to increase productivity. The new at the heart of the creative dispositif is not something *altogether other*. Paradoxically, it continues the same. It therefore does not bring forth a new form of life that goes beyond production and consumption. In the neoliberal performance society, the new, novelty, is ultimately a form of consumption.

Classical modernity's emphasis on the radically new is alien to the postmodern creative dispositif. In classical modernity, people strove to be 'starting from the very beginning', to 'begin by clearing a tabula rasa'. Walter Benjamin mentions a number of modern artists and writers who were inspired by 'starting from the very beginning'. They resolutely turned away from the musty bourgeoisie and turned instead 'to the naked man of the contemporary world who lies screaming like a newborn babe in the dirty diapers of the present'.[13] The postmodern creative dispositif is not on its way towards a new birth. It lacks the pathos of the new, the passion for the new. It produces only *variations of the same*.

Self-creation, creative self-realization, also has something compulsive about it. We optimize ourselves, exploit ourselves, to the bitter end, while harbouring the illusion that we are realizing ourselves. These inner compulsions intensify fear, and ultimately make us depressive. Self-creation is a form of self-exploitation that serves the purpose of increasing productivity.

Digital communication heightens people's isolation. Paradoxically, social media undermines sociability. It leads, ultimately, to an erosion of social coherence. Although we are extremely well connected, we are not *united*. Relationships are replaced by contacts. There is no *touching*. We live in a *touchless society*. Unlike physical touch, contact does not create *closeness*. When the other, the thou, becomes a mere 'it' that satisfies my needs or bolsters my ego, the relationship to the other withers. The other in whom I see myself reflected loses its otherness, its alterity. Society's growing narcissism, which leads to the absence of attachment and touch, deepens fear.

Hope is a counter-figure, even a *counter-mood*, to fear: rather than isolating us, it *unites and forms communities*. Gabriel Marcel writes: '"I hope in thee for us"; such is perhaps the most adequate and the most elaborate expression of the act which the verb "to hope" suggests in a way which is still confused and ambiguous.'[14] He also remarks that hope 'appears to us as inspired by love, or perhaps more exactly by a combination of scenes which this love conjures up and irradiates'.[15] Fear and love are mutually exclusive. Hope, by contrast, includes love. Hope does not isolate. It reconciles, unites, and forms bonds. Fear agrees with neither trust nor community, with neither closeness nor touch. It leads to alienation, loneliness, isolation, forlornness, helplessness and distrust.

Ernst Bloch, in *The Principle of Hope*, claims that, like virtue, hope 'is teachable'; it can be learned. Early in the introduction, he says: 'Once a man travelled far and wide to learn fear. In the time that has just passed, it came easier and closer, the art was mastered in a terrible fashion. But now . . . a feeling that suits us better is overdue.' And the next paragraph continues: 'It is a question of learning hope.'[16] But hope cannot be taught or learned in the way that virtue can. In a climate of fear, there is no hope. Fear represses hope. What is needed is therefore a

politics of hope that creates an *atmosphere* of hope against *the regime of fear*.[17]

Fear isolates people, so collective fear is impossible. Fear does not create a *community*, a *We*. In fear, everyone is by him- or herself, in isolation. Hope, by contrast, contains a dimension of *We*. To hope means 'to *spread* hope', *to carry the torch*, 'keeping its flame a radiance of hope burning around one'.[18] Hope is the catalyst of revolution, the catalyst of the new: *incipit vita nova* [Here begins the new life]. There is no *revolution through fear*. The fearful submit to domination. Revolution can only come about through a hope for another, better world. Today, revolution is impossible because we cannot *hope*, because we are paralysed by fear, because life deteriorates into survival.

Today's depressed and hopeless society is reflected in the dystopian science-fiction film *Children of Men*. The film depicts humankind as approaching its end, threatened by extinction. For reasons that are unclear, no woman has become pregnant for the last eighteen years. The youngest person on earth, eighteen-year-old 'Baby Diego', is killed in the film's opening scene. The world is shaken by violence, terror, chaos, xenophobia and environmental disaster. If the good news of the Christmas story, 'A child has been born unto us', is a message of hope, mankind's sterility represents complete hopelessness. Miraculously, a woman becomes pregnant. She is meant to be brought to a secret place where scientists undertake research in the hope of securing humanity's continued existence. In the final scene, the pregnant character, Kee – played, fittingly, by Clare-Hope Ashitey – is saved from distress in rough seas by a ship named *Tomorrow*.

Mark Fisher says of the film:

> *Children of Men* connects with the suspicion that the end has already come, the thought that it could well be the case that the future harbors only reiteration and re-permutation. Could it be that there are no breaks, no 'shocks of the new' to come? Such anxieties tend to result in a bi-polar oscillation: the 'weak messianic' hope that there must be something new on the way lapses into the morose conviction that nothing new can ever happen.[19]

In *Children of Men*, humanity falls into collective depression. The act of birth, a synonym for a future whose task is to create the *new*, no longer takes place. The coming-into-the-world, giving birth, is altogether undone. The world resembles a hell of the same. Depression robs humanity of all hope. The depressed, exhausted future consists of the constant repetition of the same. Nothing *opens up. Nothing new enters the world.* The invigorating, encouraging, inspiring future, that is, '*l'avenir*', is entirely absent. No departure, no tomorrow, no *incipit vita nova*, no escape from the same, from the old, seems possible. Depression is the exact opposite of hope, which is *passion for the new*. Hope is the spring, the zest, that liberates us from our depression, from an exhausted future.

Hope and Acting

Since antiquity, hope has been juxtaposed with action. Hope lacks the determination to act – so goes the well-known criticism. The hopeful do not act. They close their eyes to reality. It is said that hope serves mainly to create illusion and distract people from the present, from life here and now. This is also Albert Camus's view: 'the fatal evasion . . . is hope. Hope of another life . . . or trickery of those who live not for life itself but for some great idea that will transcend it, refine it, give it a meaning, and betray it.'[1] Camus equates hope with resignation, with not-wanting-to-live, with the rejection of life:

From the mass of human evils swarming in Pandora's box, the Greeks brought out hope at the very last, as the most terrible of all. I don't know any symbol more moving. For hope, contrary to popular belief, is tantamount to resignation. And to live is not to be resigned.[2]

Contra Camus, hope remained inside Pandora's box. It did not get out. In this way, hope might be understood as the antidote to all of humankind's ills. As a remedy, it is still hidden. It cannot simply be found. It ensures that, despite all the ills of the world, we *do not resign ourselves*. For Nietzsche, hope is a determined *'yes to life'*, an 'and yet': 'For what Zeus wanted was that man, however much tormented by the other evils, should nonetheless not throw life away but continue to let himself be tormented. To that end he gives men hope.'[3]

What actually is this 'life itself' or 'life as such' (*la vie même*) that hope allegedly 'evades', or even 'betrays'? Is it nutritional life, which merely feeds itself? Is a 'life as such' that gets by without anything 'ideational', without any 'meaning', even conceivable or desirable? Freedom, without which action in the proper sense is impossible, is already an idea that provides meaning. Without ideas, without a horizon of meaning, life withers and becomes *survival*, or – as we see today – the *pure immanence of consumption. Consumers have no hope.* All they have are wishes or needs. Nor do they need a future. When consumption becomes total, time withers. It turns into a constant present of needs and their satisfaction. Hope is not part of capitalism's vocabulary. *Those who hope do not consume.*

Camus has an overly narrow conception of hope. According to his conception, hope does not have a dimension of 'action'. This utterly fails to recognize the active dimension of hope, that aspect of it that motivates us to act and inspires us to create the new. Without hope, 'man's desperate effort to turn his most perspicacious dreams into reality' will be in vain.[4] And the most perspicacious dreams are *daydreams of hope*. According to Camus, the inescapable absurdity of human existence gives rise to a longing for home, a yearning for a place of belonging: 'My reasoning wants to be faithful to the evidence that aroused it. That evidence is the absurd. It is that divorce between the mind that desires and the world that disappoints, my nostalgia for unity.'[5] If, for Camus, 'a man's thought is nostalgia', then hope is necessarily inherent in thinking.[6] Hope is a form of longing. A thinking that is devoid of any hope is ultimately a calculating. It does not create anything new; it does not create a future.

In *The Myth of Sisyphus*, Camus describes a futureless passion that focuses exclusively on the present:

> All that remains is a fate whose outcome alone is fatal. Outside of that single fatality of death, everything, joy or happiness, is liberty. A world remains of which man is the sole master. What bound him was the illusion of another world. The outcome of his thought, ceasing to be renunciatory, flowers in images. It frolics – in myths, to be sure, but myths with no other depth than that of human suffering and, like it, inexhaustible. Not the divine fable that amuses and blinds, but the terrestrial face, gesture, and drama in which are summed up a difficult wisdom and an ephemeral passion [*une passion sans lendemain*].[7]

A dreamless present does not create anything new. It lacks a passion for the new, for possibility, for new beginnings. There can be no future without passion. A present reduced to nothing but itself, without a tomorrow or

future, is not the temporality of a resolute action that is determined to bring about a new beginning. Rather, it deteriorates into *the mere optimization of what is already there, even of the falsely existing*. Without any horizon to provide meaning, action becomes impossible. Happiness, freedom, wisdom, philanthropy, friendship, humanity and solidarity, all of which Camus frequently invokes, form a horizon of meaning against which action makes sense and finds orientation. How else should we understand Camus's talk of his 'fidelity to a light in which I was born, and in which for thousands of years men have learned to welcome life even in suffering'?[8] *Light always comes from above.*

In his acceptance speech upon receiving the Nobel Prize for Literature, Camus seems to allow his theoretical strictures to loosen, and an idea of hope that he never pursued in his philosophical writing seems to impose itself on him. Against his will, he invokes an altogether different hope: 'the faint sound of beating wings' and 'the sweet stirrings of life and hope'.[9] Here, hope is no longer resignation, avoidance or the renunciation of life; it is life itself, *la vie même*. Life and hope become one. *To live means to hope.*

Spinoza also considered hope to be irrational. Whoever acts under 'the guidance of reason' needs neither hope nor fear. Reason and hope are set up as opposites. Proposition XLVII of Part 4 of *Ethics* says: 'The emotions of hope and fear cannot be good of themselves.'[10] In the note to the proposition, Spinoza adds:

In proportion, therefore, as we endeavor to live according to the guidance of reason, shall we strive as much

22

as possible to depend less on hope, to liberate ourselves from fear, to rule fortune, and to direct our actions by the sure counsels of reason.[11]

Spinoza rules out the possibility that hope could open up a space for action that is not accessible to reason. However, hope builds a bridge across the abyss into which reason cannot look. It can hear an *undertone* to which reason is deaf. Reason does not recognize the signs of *what is coming, what is not yet born*. Reason is an organ that detects *what is already there*.

The conventional criticism of hope ignores its complexity and inner tensions. Hope goes far beyond passive expectations and wishes. Hope's fundamental traits are enthusiasm and motivation – it is a spring. It is even 'a militant emotion' that 'unfurls banners'.[12] Inherent in it is a determination to act. It develops *forces* that make people *spring into action*. We must distinguish between two kinds of hope: a passive, inactive and weak sort and an active, acting and strong one. It is true that passive hope approximates the vain wish. *Active and strong hope*, however, inspires people to creative action.

A wish or expectation relates to an object or inner-worldly event. They are *point-like*. Hope, by contrast, develops a *narrative* that guides action. It is characterized by narrative length and breadth. Unlike a wish, hope stimulates the narrative imagination. It *actively dreams*. A wish necessarily involves a feeling of lack, whereas hope possesses a *fullness* and *luminosity of its own*. Strong hope does not lack anything. '*Effervescent hope*' is not an oxymoron. Hope is a *force*, a *momentum*. A wish, by contrast, is never *forceful*.

To the hopeful, the world appears in a different light. Hope gives the world a special *radiance*; it *brightens* the world. Wishes or expectations do not possess this power to change, open up or brighten the world. They simply await the inner-worldly events or objects that satisfy them. Fulfilment and satisfaction are alien to hope. Hope is not bound up with an object or inner-worldly event. It is a *mood*, even a *fundamental mood*, that *thoroughly attunes* [be-*stimmt*] human existence.[13] If it is intensified, it can even become an *elated mood*. Terry Eagleton completely ignores this active dimension of hope when he writes:

> To speak hopefully is to use words in a certain way, not to invest them with a particular affect. Even if one privately feels nothing but a spasm of savage nihilism in the act of consoling someone else, hopeful words remain hopeful words. ... One may recognise that a hope is real without having the least sensation of it. ... To ask 'What do you hope to achieve?' is to request an account of a project, not a report on a subjective condition. ... Like any virtue, it is an acquired habit of thinking, feeling and acting in a specific way.[14]

As a mood, a fundamental mood, hope is *pre-linguistic*. It *attunes* [be-*stimmt*] language. Hope, experienced in its highest intensity, cannot be a habit or virtue that we acquire or consciously bring about. Inherent in it is a transcendence that exceeds the immanence of the will. As a mood, anxiety, too, lies beyond our will.[15] It overcomes us. A mood differs categorically from a habit. Habits do not form quickly. By contrast, we are simply *put* into moods. We *fall* into them. They can *ambush*, *capture* and *transform* us.

In *Philosophical Investigations*, Wittgenstein asks an interesting question: 'One can imagine an animal angry, fearful, sad, joyful, startled. But hopeful? And why not?' Wittgenstein gives himself the following answer to this speculative question:

> A dog believes his master is at the door. But can he also believe that his master will come the day after tomorrow? – And *what* can he not do here? – How do I do it? – What answer am I supposed to give to this?
>
> Can only those hope who can talk? Only those who have mastered the use of a language. That is to say, the manifestations of hope are modifications of this complicated form of life.[16]

We cannot deny animals all linguistic capacity. However, the language of animals has an altogether different temporal structure from that of human language. It lacks the future tense in the proper sense. Hope inhabits the future. To the extent that it can use signs that bear meanings, an animal can speak. But it cannot make a *promise*. The language of animals is also not narrative. They cannot *narrate*. Animals may well have wishes, but unlike a wish, hope has a narrative structure. Narration presupposes a significant temporal awareness. An animal cannot develop the idea of a *tomorrow*, because this idea has a narrative character. An animal has no access to a *narrative future*.

Hope has an *active core*. The spirit of hope invigorates and spurs us to action. Erich Fromm writes about the active, strong and determined kind of hope:

Hope is paradoxical. It is neither passive waiting nor is it unrealistic forcing of circumstances that cannot occur. It is like a crouched tiger, which will jump only when the moment for jumping has come. . . . To hope means to be ready at every moment for that which is not yet born . . . Those whose hope is strong see and cherish all signs of new life and are ready every moment to help the birth of that which is ready to be born.[17]

Hope looks ahead and anticipates. It affords us a power to act and perceive of which neither reason nor understanding are capable. Hope sharpens our sense for what-is-not-yet, the not-yet-born that dawns at the horizon of the future. It is the *midwife of the new*. Without hope, there can be no *departure* or *revolution*. Indeed, it is quite possible that evolution is driven by unconscious hope. Hope is the invigorating force *per se*, which innervates life and protects it against torpor and paralysis. According to Fromm, hope – as a 'state of being', as a mood – is an 'inner readiness, that of intense but not-yet-spent activeness'.[18] In this way, it is an inner source of activity and action. It takes us beyond spent activity, beyond mere hustle and bustle, and brings us into contact with *not-yet-spent activeness*, with the *freshness of the not-yet-born*. It *rejuvenates* our actions.

Following Nietzsche, we may understand hope as a specific state of mind that is akin to *pregnancy*. To hope means *to be ready for the birth of the new*:

Is there a more holy condition than that of pregnancy? To do all we do in the unspoken belief that it has somehow to benefit that which is coming to be within us!

26

– has to enhance its mysterious worth, the thought of which fills us with delight! In this condition we avoid many things without having to force ourself very hard! We suppress our anger, we offer the hand of conciliation: our child shall grow out of all that is gentlest and best. We are horrified if we are sharp or abrupt: suppose it should pour a drop of evil into the dear unknown's cup of life! Everything is veiled, ominous, we know nothing of what is taking place, we wait and try to be ready. At the same time, a pure and purifying feeling of profound irresponsibility reigns in us almost like that of the auditor before the curtain has gone up – it is growing, it is coming to light: we have no right to determine either its value or the hour of its coming. All the influence we can exert lies in keeping it safe. 'What is growing here is something greater than we are' is our most secret hope.[19]

In hoping, we lift ourselves above the badly existing. We *forgive* it, expecting something altogether other. *Forgiveness* prepares the soil for the new, for what is other.

Hope brings with it a great mildness, a serene calmness, even a deep *friendliness*, because it does not enforce anything. In Nietzsche's fitting words, it is a proud and mild mood. To hope means to be *intensely prepared for what is to come*. Hope increases our sensibility for *what-is-not-yet*, on which we have no direct influence. Even thinking and acting have this *contemplative* dimension of hoping, that is, of receiving, of presentiment, of waiting, of granting and letting happen. Pure action is *without consecration*. At the core of the highest form of activity there is an *element of inactivity*. Hope introduces us into that realm of being that escapes our will. Willing cannot reach the seed of creation:

> It is in this state of consecration that one should live! It is a state one can live in! And if what is expected is an idea, a deed – towards every bringing forth we have essentially no other relationship than that of pregnancy and ought to blow to the winds all presumptuous talk of 'willing' and 'creating'.[20]

Martin Luther King nicely conveys the active aspect of hope. In his famous 'I Have a Dream' speech, he says:

> With this faith, we will be able to hew out of the mountain of despair, a stone of hope. With this faith, we will be able to transform the jangling discords of our nation into a beautiful symphony of brotherhood. With this faith we will be able to work together, to pray together, to struggle together, to go to jail together, to stand up for freedom together, knowing that we will be free one day.[21]

The fact that the mountain of despair precedes the stone of hope shows that King is not an optimist. His dream is a daydream. Daydreams are born out of hope. Hope stimulates us to imagine new forms of action. To be sure, there are also daydreams that flee from reality and quickly melt into thin air. These are much like illusions or wishful thinking. Active hope, by contrast, nourishes those daydreams that are anchored in reality, that form and create the future. Active hope is expressed in a refusal to put up with the badly existing. In its daydreams, this kind of hope is *determined to act*. Daydreams are ultimately *dreams of action*. They dream away the badly existing in the interest of a new and better life.

Daydreams depict what is coming, what is-not-yet, what is-not-yet-born. They face towards the future, whereas night-dreams reveal the past. Daydreams dream forward, whereas night-dreams dream backwards:

> we find repeatedly: that which is exclusively repressed downwards and to be found in the subconscious is in reality only the soil from which night-dreams emerge and occasionally the poison which causes neurotic symptoms ... Whereas that which is hoped for and imagined contains the possible treasure from which the great daylight fantasies are derived.[22]

Whereas for Freud daydreams are the mere precursors of night-dreams,[23] Bloch takes daydreams to be independent entities. The ego of night-dreams is introverted, immersed in itself. It does not open itself up to others:

> The ego of the waking dream may become so extensive that it represents others along with it. Thus we reach the third point where daydreams and night-dreams differ: human breadth makes them different. The sleeper is alone with his treasures, the ego of the enthuser can refer to others. If the ego is no longer introverted in such a way or does not only refer to its immediate environment, then its daydream wants to improve publicly. Even still privately rooted dreams of this kind apply themselves to what is inside only because they want to improve it in collaboration with other egos.[24]

Night-dreams do not motivate us to act collectively. In night-dreams, everyone is isolated.

Daydreams, by contrast, suggest a *We* that is ready to act to improve the world. Only daydreamers are capable of revolution.

Daydreams have a political dimension and a utopian potential, whereas night-dreams do not go beyond the private. Beauty, sublimity and transfiguration are possible only in daydreams. Night-dreams lack utopian breadth and momentum. They are disinclined to act. Revolutionaries dream during the day. They *dream forward*, and they do so together. Dreams about how to improve the world are daydreams brought about by strong hope. Night-dreams have no place for hope. They are usually *dreams about wishes or fears*. According to Freud, the function of dreams is to come to terms with past traumata. Night-dreams do not have a future dimension.

In *The Human Condition*, Hannah Arendt remarks that 'faith and hope' are 'thosetwo essential characteristics of human existence which Greek antiquity ignored altogether, discounting the keeping of faith as a very uncommon and not too important virtue and counting hope among the evils of illusion in Pandora's box'.[25] Despite making hope one of the essential traits of human existence, Arendt, oddly, does not elaborate on it. Arendt's *The Human Condition* lacks a theory of hope. Hope is not given an essential role in connection with action.

According to Arendt, acting means beginning something new on one's own initiative. Having been born, human beings are new arrivals in the world, so they can take the initiative and get something new going.

But human action is characterized by radical contingency. Humans can begin something new, but they are altogether incapable of controlling it or predicting its consequences. When acting, no one quite knows what they are doing. According to Arendt, human action creates guilt; the actor 'becomes "guilty" of consequences he never intended or even foresaw ... no matter how disastrous and unexpected the consequences of his deed he can never undo it'.[26] Humans must therefore bear the burden of the irreversibility and unpredictability of the consequences of their actions.

In the face of this unavoidable *guilt*, Arendt introduces 'forgiveness' into her argument. Forgiveness pardons the guilt inherent in action. It ensures that we can mutually acquit one another for the consequences of our actions. For Arendt, forgiveness is a 'remedy' for the irreversibility and unpredictability of the process set in train by action, for the fact that we cannot undo what we have done.[27] Only the faculty of forgiveness can put us in a position to 'remain free agents': 'only by constant willingness to change their minds and start again can they be trusted with so great a power as that to begin something new'.[28]

Forgiveness relates to the past by undoing what happened and thus creating free space for a new beginning. But we act into an uncertain future. This contingency, owed to the futurity within every act, forgiveness cannot control. The unreliability and inscrutability of the human heart creates a fog of uncertainty. The unforeseeability of the future is the context in which Arendt introduces the idea of the 'promise'. Promises are 'isolated islands of certainty in an ocean of uncertainty'.[29] They allow us 'to dispose of the future as though it were the present'.[30] A promise thus makes the future predictable and disposable. Arendt quotes Nietzsche, who referred to the 'awareness of power and freedom' gained by the one 'who gives his word as something that can be relied on, because he is strong enough to remain upright in the face of mishap or even "in the face of fate"'.[31]

If forgiveness makes the past *manageable*, a promise does this for the future. According to Arendt, forgiving and promising are two fundamental conditions of human action. They are, she says, 'like control mechanisms built into the very faculty to start new and unending processes'.[32]

'Without the faculty to undo what we have done and to control at least partially the processes we have let loose', we could not act. And if we could not act, our lives could 'only follow the law of mortality, which is the most certain and the only reliable law of a life spent between birth and death'.[33] The automatic process of life is interrupted only by the capacity to act. Without 'the faculty of beginning something anew', the 'life span of man running toward death would inevitably carry everything human to ruin and destruction'.[34]

According to Arendt, the automatic processes that determine the course of the world are such that every human action takes on the character of a miracle:

Action is, in fact, the one miracle-working faculty of man, as Jesus of Nazareth . . . must have known very well when he likened the power to forgive to the more general power of performing miracles, putting both on the same level and within the reach of man.[35]

33

The miracle that repeatedly interrupts the course of the world and saves it from ruin is, according to Arendt, the 'fact of natality', of 'being born'. In this fact, 'the faculty of action is ontologically rooted'. Only at this point does Arendt begin to speak of hope. The miracle is,

> in other words, the birth of new men and the new beginning, the action they are capable of by virtue of being born. Only the full experience of this capacity can bestow upon human affairs faith and hope . . . It is this faith in and hope for the world that found perhaps its most glorious and most succinct expression in the few words with which the Gospels announced their 'glad tidings': 'A child has been born unto us.'[36]

These are the rough outlines of Arendt's theory of action. For her, hope is not an essential part of action. Humans can hope only because they can act. For action as such, hope is irrelevant. In this way, Arendt fails to acknowledge the primordial nature of hope, which transforms it into a driving force for action. In fact, hope precedes action, not vice versa. It is not action but hope that brings about *miracles*.

It seems that the contemplative aspects internal to hope prevent Arendt from integrating hope into her theory of action. Despite hope's proximity to action, hope does not belong to the sphere of *vita activa*. Arendt is fundamentally suspicious of contemplation. Her concept of action relates exclusively to activity, to deliberately taken initiative. Arendt thus fails to appreciate the fact that, in hope, *vita activa* and *vita contemplativa* enter into a beautiful synthesis.

Humans can act *because* they can hope. New beginnings are impossible without hope. The spirit of hope inspires action. It gives action a *passion for the new*. Action thereby becomes *passion*. Someone who does not *dream ahead* does not dare to embark on a new beginning. Without the spirit of hope, action withers; it becomes pure activity or problem-solving.

Hope looks for *salvation*. The glad tiding 'A child has been born unto us' is a genuine expression of hope. Hope does not relate to action. It precedes it. In Christmas oratorios, faith and hope cause jubilation:

> Triumph, rejoicing, rise, praising these days now,
> Tell ye what this day the Highest hath done!
> Fear now abandon and banish complaining,
> Join, filled with triumph and gladness, our song![37]

Arendt's theory of forgiveness does not do justice to the phenomenon. I cannot be forgiven for what I did not explicitly want to happen. I cannot ask to be forgiven for the unintended consequences of my deeds. They derive from the contingency of action, for which no one can be made responsible. At this point, we confront an *ontological guilt* for which there is no forgiveness. This guilt expresses the finitude of human existence, of human freedom. To be guilty, in this context, means that human beings are exposed to the consequences of their actions and that these consequences escape the control of our free will. Only an absolute and infinitely free God who can take control of all consequences of his actions could be innocent.

Heidegger captures the finite nature of human existence – which is grounded in the fact that humans do not themselves establish the ground of their being – in the term 'being-guilty'. For this ontological guilt, there is no forgiveness. Forgiveness relates to a deliberate action and is *independent of the action's unforeseeable consequences*. Contingency is not an object of forgiveness. It is *not forgiveness but hope that opens up a space of freedom and new beginnings*. Hope ensures that we knowingly disregard the negative consequences of the processes set in motion by our actions and regain our openness towards what might be *possible*. In hope, we bid farewell to the past and look towards the future, towards what is possible and what-is-not-yet.

Hope presupposes an open future, which also implies unintended and unforeseeable *events* that cannot be controlled in advance. If we use the power of the promise *to close down* time altogether, that is, if we 'dispose of the future as though it were the present', hope becomes superfluous. Like hope, trust presupposes an *open* horizon. To trust someone means to build a positive relationship with that person despite a lack of knowledge of the future. Trust enables action in the absence of knowledge. Knowledge, by contrast, makes trust superfluous. Arendt, however, claims that 'the force of mutual promise' is ultimately translated into the form of the 'contract'.[38] A contract is based not on trust or on a promise but on violence. Where there is absolute trust or an absolute promise, a contract is superfluous. A contract involves violence insofar as it threatens penalties or sanctions for its violation. We enter into a contract because we cannot trust. Trust excludes the possibility of violence. A law on which we agree also has a contractual character. It is precisely the threat of the use of violence that forces the partners entering into a contract to abide by it, and likewise to abide by a law. A contract radically removes the space of trust. We have to rely on trust because we cannot determine all relations between humans in legal terms. Trust facilitates social interaction.

Most importantly, Arendt's interpretation of the 'glad tidings' eliminates its *eschatological* dimension. The place of Christian hope is not immanent action but *transcendent faith*. Jürgen Moltmann writes in his *Theology of Hope*:

> The Christian hope is directed towards a *novum ultimum*, towards a new creation of all things by the God of the resurrection of Jesus Christ. It thereby opens a future outlook that embraces all things, including also death, and into this it can and must also take the limited hopes of a renewal of life, stimulating them, relativizing them, giving them direction.[39]

Christian hope does not lead to idle passivity. Rather, it pushes people to action by stimulating them to imagine new ways of acting, and by arousing 'inventiveness . . . in breaking with the old and coming to terms with the new'.[40] This hope does not 'flee the world'; it 'strains after the future'.[41] Its essence is not a quietist withdrawal but the 'cor inquietum', the restless heart. Hope neither leaves out nor leaves aside the world. Rather, it confronts the world in its full negativity and files its *objections*. Thus, it nourishes the *spirit of revolution*. 'Always the Christian hope has had a revolutionary effect in this sense on the intellectual history of the society affected by it.'[42] The determination to act is inherent in the spirit of hope. Whoever hopes *is inspired by the new*, by the *novum ultimum*. Hope dares to take the *leap towards a new life*.

Absolute hope arises in the face of the *negativity of absolute despair*. It germinates close to the *abyss*. The negativity of absolute despair characterizes a situation in which action seems no longer possible. It germinates in the moment of the total collapse of the narrative that constitutes our life. The narrative consists of meaningful relations that determine what is good, what is beautiful, what makes sense, what is valuable or desirable. The total collapse of the narrative destroys the world, life, that is, all values and norms we use for our orientation. This radical collapse means a *collapse of language*, even *of the concepts* with which a given life can be described and understood.

Action is possible only within a texture of meaning. If this texture unravels, all that is possible is meaning-less doing or blind activity. What can save us from this absolute despair? This is not just a question of solving a problem or resolving a conflict. Problems are deficiencies or dysfunctions within an otherwise sound life; they can be rectified and well-being restored [Wiederherstellung des Heils]. But if the coherence of life itself hopelessly collapsed [heillos zusammenbricht], we would *not even* have problems to be solved. In this situation, the solution [*Lösung*] of problems cannot liberate us from the absolute negativity of despair – only *salvation* [*Erlösung*] could do that.

The deeper the despair, the more intense the hope. That is the *dialectic of hope*. The negativity of despair deepens hope. The higher hope soars, the deeper its roots. In this, it differs from optimism. Optimism lacks negativity. Amid deep despair, absolute hope makes action possible again. Absolute hope involves an unshakeable belief that there is a *sense* in things. It is only this belief in *sense* that gives us orientation and puts us on a sure footing.

For Paul Celan, hope means 'not being forlorn'. However, the firm belief in 'not being forlorn' arises only in the face of total loss, of total forlornness. Like deep happiness, hope *can exist only in a broken form*. A *brokenness* is inherent in hope. The *negativity of fracture* inspires hope. Paradoxically, the bright light of hope feeds off the deepest darkness. Optimism involves no such dialectic.

For Paul Celan, language is an important space of hope that asserts itself against terrifying silence, against frightening muteness:

> Only one thing remained reachable, close and not forlorn amid all losses: language. Yes, language. In spite of everything, it remained secure against loss. But it had to go through its own lack of answers, through terrifying silence, through the thousand darknesses of murderous speech. It went through. It gave me no words for what was happening, but went through it. Went through and could resurface, 'enriched' by it all.[43]

An 'and yet' is inherent in hope. It *defies* even *absolute disaster*. The *star of hope* is a neighbour of the unlucky star (Latin: *des-astrum*). Without the negativity of disaster and the defiant attitude of 'and yet', there is only the banality of optimism. In Ingeborg Bachmann, the negativity of hope is condensed into an *'and yet'*. Language and poetry, in particular, represent this *'and yet'*. *As long as poets speak, there remains hope in the world*:

I actually do believe in something, and I call it 'a day will come'. And one day it will come – well, most likely it will not come because it has always been destroyed for us. For so many thousand years, it has always been destroyed. It will not come, *and yet* I believe in it because if I don't believe in it, I cannot go on writing either.[44]

Hope is a catalyst for writing. Poetry is a language of hope.

Bachmann elevates hope to a *condition of the possibility of living*. Hope represents the *conditio humana* as such. Hope is what guides human action. On this point, Bachmann differs radically from Arendt. For Arendt action has the highest priority; for Bachmann it comes after hope. Hope is what provides the motivation needed to bridge the gulf to action. *Humans live as long as they hope*. Bachmann always emphasizes the *paradoxical, aporetic* character of hope:

'Bohemia Lies by the Sea' is for me the one poem by which I shall always stand. It is directed at all human beings because it is the land of their hope which they shall never reach, *and yet* hope they must because other-wise they could not live. . . . It is a utopia, that is, a land that does not exist because Bohemia, obviously, does not lie by the sea, as, after all, we know very well. But it lies by the sea after all. . . . That means it is something incommensurable. . . . And for me someone who does not hope, and who does not live, and who does not love, and who does not hope to get to this land, is not a human being.[45]

The tension between the impossible and the 'and yet', an act of faith, opens up the future, sustains language. An 'and yet' makes life possible.

Bachmann soaks her poem 'Bohemia Lies by the Sea' in green, gives it the colour of hope:

> If the houses here are green, I'll step inside a house.
> If the bridges here are strong, I'll walk on solid ground.

Hope makes *housing* possible. It promises a *house*, a *home-land*. Hope builds a *bridge* across the impassable, the abyss. Hope gives us *orientation* and a *sure footing*. Someone who hopes walks 'on solid ground'. Bachmann holds on to Celan's notion of 'not being forlorn'. Paradoxically, we reach solid ground when we face ruin. Being lost and not being forlorn strengthen each other:

> If love's labor is lost in every age, I'd like to lose it here.
> . . . I want nothing more for myself. Let me go under
>   now.
> Underground – that means the ocean, there I'll find
>   Bohemia again.
> From my ruins I wake up in peace.
> From deep down I know, and am not lost.[46]

In one of his parables, Franz Kafka illustrates *hope against all hope*. The parable's protagonist is tellingly called 'Hopeless':

> Hopeless was voyaging round the Cape of Good Hope
> in a little boat. It was early in the morning, a strong wind
> was blowing. Hopeless hoisted a little sail and leaned

back tranquilly. What should he fear in the little boat, which with its tiny draught glided over all the reefs in those dangerous waters with the nimbleness of a living being?[47]

Absolute hope is a hopeless hope, or the hope of someone who is without hope, because it arises in the face of total hopelessness. We wrest it from the negativity of absolute despair. It is characterized by a resolute 'and yet'. As a permanent *condition of existence*, it is not on its way towards a specific target or nearby harbour. Kafka's 'Hopeless' *does not arrive. Not-arriving* is the fundamental trait of absolute hope. Absolute hope affords composure and confidence to life. Thus, moving in dangerous waters, Kafka's 'Hopeless' leans back tranquilly.

Negativity is essential to hopeless hope. In Letter to the Romans, St Paul says of Abraham that he 'against hope believed in hope'.[48] The more hopeless the situation, the firmer the hope. Kafka's parable 'An Imperial Message' also expresses the negativity of hope:

The Emperor, so a parable runs, has sent a message to you, the humble subject, the insignificant shadow cowering in the remotest distance before the imperial sun; the Emperor from his deathbed has sent a message to you alone. He has commanded the messenger to kneel down by the bed, and has whispered the message to him; so much store did he lay on it that he ordered the messenger to whisper it back into his ear again. Then by a nod of the head he has confirmed that it is right. Yes, before the assembled spectators of his death – all the obstructing walls have been broken down, and on the

spacious and loftily mounting open staircases stand in a ring the great princes of the Empire – before all these he has delivered his message. The messenger immediately sets out on his journey; a powerful, an indefatigable man; now pushing with his right arm, now with his left, he cleaves a way for himself through the throng; if he encounters resistance he points to his breast, where the symbol of the sun glitters; the way is made easier for him than it would be for any other man. But the multitudes are so vast; their numbers have no end. If he could reach the open fields how fast he would fly, and soon doubtless you would hear the welcome hammering of his fists on your door. But instead how vainly does he wear out his strength; still he is only making his way through the chambers of the innermost palace; never will he get to the end of them; and if he succeeded in that nothing would be gained; he must next fight his way down the stair; and if he succeeded in that nothing would be gained; the courts would still have to be crossed; and after the courts the second outer palace; and once more stairs and courts; and once more another palace; and so on for thousands of years; and if at last he should burst through the outermost gate – but never, never can that happen – the imperial capital would lie before him, the center of the world, crammed to bursting with its own sediment. Nobody could fight his way through here even with a message from a dead man. But you sit at your window when evening falls and dream it to yourself.[49]

As long as the dream continues, the imperial message is on its way to the chosen recipient. It is ultimately hope that creates or dreams the message.

The parable is embedded in Kafka's story 'The Great Wall of China', which is also about hopeless hope, namely the seemingly impossible task of completing the Great Wall. It speaks of the 'hopelessness of such hard toil, which yet could not reach completion in the longest lifetime'.[50] But hopeless hope keeps the building going. Following the parable of the imperial message, the text continues: 'Just so, as hopelessly and as hopefully, do our people regard the Emperor.'[51] Absolute hope is an endless process. The imperial message does not arrive. It is this not-arriving that sustains hope.

The endless building of the wall creates a stable community by uniting the whole people in the spirit of hope. The wall is not really for the protection of the people against external enemies. The suspicion is that the 'people of the north', against whom the wall is allegedly meant to protect the Chinese, do not actually exist:

> We have not seen them, and if we remain in our villages we shall never see them, even if on their wild horses they should ride as hard as they can straight toward us – the land is too vast and would not let them reach us, they would end their course in the empty air.[52]

If there are no enemies, what protection does the wall provide? The building of the wall strengthens the *internal* coherence of the community. In fact, it brings about the community in the genuine sense, the *collective soul*, the *pageant of the people*, in the first place. Absolute hope unites and allies the people:

> The quiet life of their homes, where they rested some time, strengthened them; the humble credulity with

which their reports were listened to, the confidence
with which the simple and peaceful burgher believed in
the eventual completion of the wall, all this filled their
hearts with a new buoyancy. Like eternally hopeful children they then said farewell to their homes; the desire
once more to labor on the wall of the nation became
irresistible. They set off earlier than they needed; half
the village accompanied them for long distances. . . .
Every fellow countryman was a brother for whom one
was building a wall of protection . . . Unity! Unity!
Shoulder to shoulder, a ring of brothers, a current of
blood no longer confined within the narrow circulation
of one body, but sweetly rolling and yet ever returning
throughout the endless leagues of China.[53]

In our narcissistic society, the movement of blood is, in
fact, limited to the narrow circulation within our egos. It
no longer flows out into the world. Worldless, we circle
around nothing but our own ego. Hope has a vastness.
It founds a *We*. In this, it differs from a wish or a simple
expectation.

In his deepest despair, Václav Havel, champion of
human rights, opponent of the communist regime in
Czechoslovakia, and later, after the collapse of the
Eastern bloc, Czechoslovakia's president, must have felt
something of absolute hope. In an interview, he made
some remarkable observations about hope:

I should probably say first that the kind of hope I often
think about (especially in situations that are particu-
larly hopeless, such as prison) I understand above all
as a state of mind . . . it is a dimension of the soul; it's

not essentially dependent on some particular observation of the world or estimate of the situation. Hope is not prognostication. It is an orientation of the spirit, an orientation of the heart; it transcends the world that is immediately experienced, and is anchored somewhere beyond its horizons. I don't think you can explain it as a mere derivative of something here, of some movement, or of some favorable signs in the world. I feel that its deepest roots are in the transcendental . . .

Hope, in this deep and powerful sense, is not the same as joy that things are going well, or willingness to invest in enterprises that are obviously headed for early success, but, rather, an ability to work for something because it is good, not just because it stands a chance to succeed. The more unpropitious the situation in which we demonstrate hope, the deeper that hope is. Hope is definitely not the same thing as optimism. It is not the conviction that something will turn out well, but the certainty that something makes sense, regardless of how it turns out. In short, I think that the deepest and most important form of hope, the only one that can keep us above water and urge us to good works, and the only true source of the breathtaking dimension of the human spirit and its efforts, is something we get, as it were, from 'elsewhere.' It is also this hope, above all, which gives us the strength to live and continually to try new things, even in conditions that seem as hopeless as ours do, here and now.[54]

For Václav Havel, hope is a 'dimension of the soul', a 'state of mind'. As an 'orientation of the spirit', it *shows the way*. It leads human beings through territory in

47

which they would normally no longer have any orientation. Havel does not locate hope in the immanent world. Rather, he assumes that it comes from *somewhere else*, from beyond the world's 'horizon'. The deepest roots of hope are in the 'transcendental'. This hope is *absolute* insofar as it is altogether independent of the immanent course of the world. It escapes all prognostication, all calculation. Havel sees himself as neither an optimist nor a pessimist, because hope has nothing to do with the way things will turn out. Hope cannot be reduced to a wish or expectation. An *auratic distance* is inherent in it. It therefore evades all disposability. It cannot be objectified into a positive wish or the satisfaction of needs.

We everywhere lose sight of what is *distant*. For this reason, we only have wishes. But we cannot hope. Without distance, there can be no nearness either. Nearness and distance condition each other. Nearness does not mean absence of distance. Distance is written into it. When distance disappears, nearness is lost, too. Nearness deepens distance. Walter Benjamin writes:

> The phenomenon of alienation … – which Kraus has formulated in the fine dictum, 'The more closely you look at a word, the more distantly it looks back' – appears to extend to the optical. At any rate, I find among my notes the surprised comment: 'How things withstand the gaze!'[55]

Distance brings language close to *poetry*. In the information society, language loses all auratic distance and becomes shallow information. Digital hyper-communication makes us *speechless*. We thus live in a time without poetry.

Someone who only consumes information no longer reads poems.

Hope transcends the immanence of human wilfulness. It reveals glimpses of what lies beyond the human. It only arises in the face of absolute negativity. The desert allows it to germinate. Paul Celan expresses the negative and transcendent character of hope in one of his poems:

THREAD SUNS
above the grey-black wilderness.
A tree-
high thought
tunes in to light's pitch: there are
still songs to be sung on the other side
of mankind.[56]

The 'grey-black wilderness' represents the negativity that is so characteristic of hope. The *tree of hope* grows in the wilderness. And hope inhabits a *far side*, a transcendence that cannot be described, that can only be *sung about*. It transcends the immanence of the purely human.

The future as an open horizon of *new, unsuspected, unprecedented* possibilities is alien to Heidegger. He holds that every world-projection remains 'within the limitations of its thrownness'.[57] Heidegger's thinking aims at essence [Wesen], at what has come about [dem Ge-Wesenen].[58] The un-born, the unprecedented [Noch-Nie-Dagewesene], has no place in this thinking. What matters is to *get back* to *what came about* [das Gewesene], that is, to the *essence*. The intentionality of *looking ahead and beyond* was unknown to Heidegger. *Back to the essence, to the past* – that is the direction in which his thinking moves.

Negativity is not an essential element in Bloch's notion of hope. For him, hope therefore comes close to the 'expectant emotion which has become absolutely positive'.[59] Bloch idealizes hope as an unshakeable, metaphysical, even cosmic principle. He talks of 'the good which is working its way through', the labouring character of which is reminiscent of Hegel's mole of history.[60] According to Bloch, hope innervates a process that could almost be called chemical, and that drives the world on to perfection:

> The substance-formations of the world – right down to the unleashing of the most intensive force of production, of the true atomic nucleus: existere, quodditas – are full of the tendency of the Not-Yet towards the All, of the alienated towards identity, of the surrounding world towards mediated homeland. . . . The hope of the goal, however, is necessarily at odds with false satisfaction, necessarily at one with revolutionary thoroughness; – crooked seeks to be straight, half to be full.[61]

In Bloch, hope is an urge towards the perfection of the world, an urge that is inherent in reality. Hope can be betrayed or misjudged, but objectively it is insistent and persistent, like a quasi-cosmic force. Terry Eagleton comments critically on the *positivity* of Bloch's notion of hope:

> If Bloch's view is valid, then it follows that hope flows with the tide of the universe rather than moving against the current. Yet if this is true, any particular act of hope

is subtly devalued. Because it partakes in the general tendency of the cosmos, it is a less arduous affair than hope *despite* – hope that refuses to give way even in the most joyless of situations.[62]

Bloch's hope lacks the '*and yet*'. It is no longer a *daring*. It is not *wrested away from* the negativity of despair. Its ubiquity is precisely what devalues it: 'Hope, to be enduring and well-founded, needs to be dearly bought, whereas one problem with Bloch's universe is that the place is awash with the stuff.'[63]

As a 'state of mind', hope cannot be disappointed, because it is independent of the immanent course that things take. Because he assumes that every hope can, even must, be disappointed, Bloch fails to recognize absolute hope, even the spirit of hope. For him, hope 'can be, and will be disappointed; indeed, it must be so, as a matter of honor, or *else it would not be hope*'. It must be 'unconditionally disappointable . . . because it is open in a forward direction, in a future-directed orientation; it does not address itself to that which already exists'.[64]

Contra Bloch, hope is, as Havel rightly points out, perfectly independent of the development of things and the development's outcome. The substance of hope is a deep conviction that something is *meaningful*, independent of any concern for whatever actual results are achieved. Hope is located in the transcendent, beyond the inner-worldly course of events. As a *faith*, it makes it possible to act amid absolute despair. The goddess of hope – Speranza – whom Orfeo invokes in the underworld, leads him through Hades, the kingdom of the dead, which represents negativity. Without Speranza, orientation in this

51

Δημητηρ ηυκομου, σεμνην. Θεαν ἄ

ον' αὐτὴν καὶ κούρην περικαλλέα
Περι...

place is impossible. Monteverdi's *L'Orfeo* transforms this *speranza assoluta* into *song*:

Corto da te, mio Nume
Speranza, unico bene
Degli afflitti mortali, omai son giunto
A questi mesti e tenebrosi regni
Ove raggio di sol giammai non giunse.
Tu, mia compagna e duce,
In cosi strane e sconosciute vie
Reggesti il passo debole e tremante,
Ond'oggi ancora spero
Di riveder quelle beate luci
Che sol'a gl'occhi miei portan il giorno.

Escorted by you, my Deity,
Hope, only solace
Given the afflicted mortals, now I have arrived
At these mournful and dark realms
Where a Sun's ray can find no entrance.
You, my companion and guide
On paths so unwonted and unknown
Have directed my feeble, trembling steps,
Where today I still hope
To see once more those blessed eyes
That alone can bring light to mine.[65]

Hope and Knowledge

Thinking has an affective, bodily dimension. *Goosebumps are the first thought image. Thought images* have deep roots in the physical body. Without feelings, emotions or affects – in general terms, without *being stirred* – there is no knowledge. Stirrings *innervate* thinking. This is precisely why artificial intelligence cannot think. Because feelings and affects are *analogue, bodily events*, they cannot be represented in algorithms. Intelligence merely calculates. It is based on *'inter-legere'*, meaning *'to choose between'*. And the choice is between *already existing* possibilities. Intelligence therefore does *not create anything new*. Someone who is capable of genuine *thought* is not intelligent. Only through thinking do we gain access to the *altogether other*. Someone who *thinks*, Deleuze would say, is an idiot. The gesture of thinking is 'faire l'idiot'.[1] Only whoever is capable of being an idiot can make a new beginning, break radically with what exists, leave the *past* in favour of what is *coming. Only idiots can hope*.

In 'Love and Knowledge', Max Scheler quotes Goethe: 'One knows nothing save what one loves, and the deeper and more complete that knowledge, the stronger and livelier must be one's love – indeed passion.'[2] According to Scheler, Pascal thought that 'love first discloses objects, which appear to the senses and which reason later judges'.[3] Although it is commonly assumed that knowledge depends on controlling one's emotional reactions, it is in fact attention, guided by love – the loving turn towards the world – that determines the steps towards knowledge, from sensory perception up to complex thought images. Pascal even wrote: 'Love and reason are one and the same.'[4] Love is not blind; it *opens our eyes*. Only lovers actually see. Love does not distort reality but reveals its *truth*. It sharpens our gaze. The stronger the love, the deeper the knowledge: 'Tantum cognoscitur, quantum diligitur.'[5] (We understand to the degree that we love.)

Love is more than merely taking an interest in and bringing into view already existing objects. Rather, it is only love that bring objects into their full existence. Scheler mentions that 'Augustine speaks in mysterious ways, for example, of the tendency of plants, when looked at by humans, to be "redeemed" in this viewing from their particular existence of being closed into themselves.'[6] It is the loving gaze that redeems flowers from their lack of being. Love affords them a *fullness of being*. Their perfection is realized in love as knowledge. The loving gaze redeems the flowers.

For Plato, love was essential to knowledge. Love – Eros – is the soul's striving for perfect knowledge. Thinking is an act of love. The philosopher is an eroticist, a lover of truth. Thinking guided by love reaches its zenith in the ecstatic beholding of the *idea of beauty* as the highest knowledge. Following Plato, Heidegger also conceives of thinking as a movement driven by Eros. Eros spurs on thinking. It gives it wings: 'I call it Eros, the oldest of the gods according to Parmenides. . . . The beat of that god's wings moves me each time I take a substantial step in my thinking and venture onto untrodden paths.'[7]

Thinking driven by Eros is a recurring motif throughout the history of philosophy. In *What is Philosophy?*, Deleuze and Guattari claim that Eros is a condition of thought. The philosopher must have been a friend, even a lover. Eros, as a *living relationship to the other*, is 'a condition of possibility of thought itself, a living category, a transcendental lived reality [*un vécu transcendental*]'.[8] A *desire for the other, for a utopian other*, is inherent to thinking. This desire is unique.

Without Eros, we remain captured in the *hell of the same*. Deleuze and Guattari ask a deep question:

What does *friend* mean when it becomes . . . a condition for the exercise of thought? Or rather, are we not talking of the lover? Does not the friend reintroduce into thought a vital relationship with the Other that was supposed to have been excluded from pure thought?[9]

Artificial intelligence lacks the capacity for thinking simply because it does not have a *friend* or a *lover*. Eros is *alien* to it. It does not feel a *desire for the other*.

Knowledge, as the *intuition of essence* [Wesensschau], is not *prospective* but *retrospective*. In *The Science of Logic*, Hegel says: 'The German language has kept "essence" (*Wesen*) in the past participle (*gewesen*) of the verb "to be" (*sein*), for essence is past – but timelessly past – being.'[10] In Plato, the acquisition of knowledge takes place in the form of a remembrance of *past* [*gewesen*] – that is, pre-existing – ideas. As the *intuition of essence*, it is turned towards the *past*. Plato's Eros does not create a buoyant movement towards the open, towards what is coming. It aims at essence, that is, at what has been. In Heidegger, the temporality of knowledge is also that of 'beenness' [*Gewesenheit*].[11] Thinking is on its way towards 'timelessly past being' as *truth*. 'Forgetfulness of being' has to be overcome by remembrance, by the re-enpresenting of being, namely by way of Eros, that is, the 'striving for being'.[12] Thinking, Heidegger says, moves 'back into something past',[13] to 'what is unable to be thought in advance' [das Unvordenkliche].[14] Thinking specifically traces what has *always already been*. The *coming*, the *unborn*, remains inaccessible to it.

Not only love but hope too produces its specific insights [*Erkenntnisse*]. Unlike love, which is turned towards the *past*, hope turns towards what is *to come*. It recognizes [*erkennt*] the not-yet-being. The temporality of hope is not beenness but the future. Its mode of knowing is not retrospective but prospective. Its '*passion for the possible*' turns the gaze towards the *not-yet-being*, towards the *unborn*.[15] Hope discloses the future possibilities of reality. Following the famous words of Anselm of Canterbury, *fides quaerens intellectum – credo, ut intelligam* (faith seeks understanding – I believe so that I may understand), Moltmann writes 'spes quaerens intellectum – spero, ut intelligam': I hope so that I may understand.[16] Hope effects a widening of the soul so that it embraces the great things: 'extensio animi ad magna'.[17] In this way, it is an outstanding medium of knowledge.

In his 1516 lecture on the Epistle to the Romans, Luther reflects on a thinking that is nourished by hope:

> The apostle philosophizes and thinks about things in a different way from the philosophers and metaphysicians. For the philosophers fix their eyes on the presence of things and reflect only on their qualities and quiddities. But the apostle drags our gaze away from their essence and attributes, and directs it towards the future. He does not speak of the essence or the workings of the creature, of *actio*, *passio* or movement, but employs a new, strange, theological term and speaks of the expectation of the creature (*expectatio creaturae*).[18]

The hopeful direct their attention not at the essence of things, at their beenness or presence (*presentiam rerum*), but at their *future*, at their future possibilities. Thinking that hopes is not articulated in *concepts* [*Begriffe*] but in *anticipations* [*Vorgriffe*] or *premonitions*. Hope opens up for us a field of possibilities. Only then can we set our eyes on a concrete goal:

> (Intimations of the future! to celebrate the future, not the past! To compose the myth of the future! To live in hope!) Blissful moments! And then to draw the curtain again and to turn our thoughts to concrete immediate goals![19]

Without hope, we remain trapped in beenness or in the badly existing. Only hope generates meaningful actions that bring the new into the world.

Moltmann remarks that thinking that hopes does not gaze at reality with the 'night eyes of Minerva's owl'.[20] It was Hegel who used Minerva's owl as a metaphor for the fact that philosophy recognizes only what has become history, that is, *beenness*:

> As the thought of the world, it appears only at a time when actuality has gone through its formative process and attained its completed state. . . . When philosophy paints its grey in grey, a shape of life has grown old, and it cannot be rejuvenated, but only recognized, by the grey in grey of philosophy; the owl of Minerva begins its flight only with the onset of dusk.[21]

Hegel denies philosophy the capacity to capture the *coming*. 'Grey in grey' is the colour of beenness. Philosophy is *re-flecting* [*Nach-Denken*], not *pro-jecting* [*Vor-Denken*]. It is not *prospective* but *retrospective*. Thinking that hopes, by contrast, looks at reality with a view to the possibilities that *have-not-yet-been*. As Karl Ludwig Michelet replied to Hegel in conversation, philosophy as pro-jecting is 'the cock's crow at a newly breaking dawn, announcing a rejuvenated shape of the world'.[22]

For messianic thinking that hopes, the past is not yet completed or frozen into the form of its beenness. The past *dreams forward* into the future, into the coming. *Essence* [*das Wesen*], *by contrast, does not dream. As been-ness*, it is completed and closed. The hopeful discover the hidden dream content of things and interpret them as *secret signs of the future*. They look at the past from the perspective of the dreamer. In awakening, their consciousness is transformed:

60

Indeed, awakening is the great exemplar of memory: the occasion on which it is given us to remember what is closest, tritest, most obvious. What Proust intends with the experimental rearrangement of furniture in matinal half-slumber, what Bloch recognizes as the darkness of the lived moment, is nothing other than what here is to be secured on the level of the historical, and collectively. There is a not-yet-conscious knowledge of what has been: its advancement has the structure of awakening.[23]

Dreaming is a method for gaining knowledge. Benjamin sends the things into a deep dream layer in order to tease out their *secret language of hope*. The significance of past things is not exhausted by what they *once were* in their original place and time. In dreaming – that is, hoping – they transcend their historical enclosure. The arcades of nineteenth-century Paris might have arisen out of industrial production and capitalism, but they contain something that is not redeemed within the capitalist-industrial order of things: 'Every epoch has such a side turned toward dreams, the child's side.'[24]

Benjamin's thinking uncovers 'the enormous energies of history that are slumbering in the "once upon a time" of classic historical narrative'.[25] In the dreams and hopes of things, Benjamin, the interpreter of dreams, sees a 'world of particular secret affinities' in which things enter into the 'most contradictory communication' and reveal an 'indeterminate affinity'.[26] This connects Benjamin to Proust. For Proust, dreams reveal the true inner life behind things. The dreamer delves into a deeper layer of being, where life incessantly spins new threads between events, creating a dense texture of relations. Truth brings about surprising encounters. It takes place the moment a dreamer 'takes two different objects, states the connexion between them . . . truth – and life too – can be attained by us only when, by comparing a quality common to two sensations, we succeed in extracting their common essence'.[27]

Sleep and dreams are privileged places of truth. They suspend the separations and delimitations that dominate wakefulness. Things reveal their truth, Proust says,

> in that thoroughly alive and creative sleep of the unconscious (a sleep in which the things that have barely touched us succeed in carving an impression, in which our sleeping hands take hold of the key that turns the lock, the key for which we have sought in vain).[28]

Hopes thus nourish dreams. *The things hope in their dreams*, or they dream because they hope. Hopes release them from their historical incarceration, because hopes disclose to them what is possible – the new, the coming, the unborn. Hopes thus salvage things and bring them into the *future*. They help things to find their deeper truth by breaking up the encrustation and solidification that historical time imposes on things. Hopes and their dreams inhabit a messianic time.

Adorno, too, conceives of hope as a *medium of truth*. For thinking that hopes, truth is not something that once was and is retrospectively brought to light, but something that first needs to be *wrested and gained* from the *false*, from the *badly existing*. The place of truth is not beenness but the future; it has a utopian, messianic core. The task of truth is to lead us out of an existence that has been recognized as false:

In the end hope, wrested from reality by negating it, is the only form in which truth appears. Without hope, the idea of truth would be scarcely even thinkable, and it is the cardinal untruth, having recognized existence to be bad, to present it as truth simply because it has been recognized.[29]

In *Minima Moralia*, Adorno states: 'Art is magic delivered from the lie of being truth.'[30] As a 'descendant of magic', whose 'taboo . . . distinguished the sacred from the everyday, seeking to keep the former pure', art now represents an 'autonomous sphere' in which the logic of the 'world as it is' does not apply. Art thus insists on the 'right to be different'.[31] It thereby opens up a *space of possibilities* in which we glimpse – as in a flash – the *premonition of a higher truth*. Hope as such has something magical about it. It does not care about the logic of the world as it is. Hope is carried by the belief that everything could radically change. Beauty, as a medium of hope that is located beyond all profane purposive rationality, illumines a *possible world* beyond what exists:

> In the magic . . . of beauty . . . the illusion of omnipotence is mirrored negatively as hope. It has escaped every trial of strength. Total purposelessness gives the lie to the totality of purposefulness in the world of domination, and only by virtue of this negation . . . has existing society up to now become aware of another that is possible.[32]

Ernst Bloch also turns away from Hegel's owl of Minerva, which follows what has been:

All knowledge, it says in *Meno*, is nothing but anamnesis, the soul remembering what it beheld in the realm of ideas before its birth . . . And it was the spell cast by this anamnesis that ensured that being – especially being as essence, *ontos*, *on* – was taken per se as having-been: essence means having-been [Wesen ist Gewesenheit]. This spell remained effective up until Hegel. It even found its culmination in Hegel, at least in the shape of his creature of dusk, Minerva; in his association of knowledge exclusively with the historical development of content; in his rejection of the open not-yet, the store of unrealized possibilities.[33]

The owl of Minerva is blind to the *dawning radiance of the new*, which escapes the logic of essence. The thinking of hope shifts knowledge's interest from the past to the future, from what has been to what is coming, and against the always-already – the temporality of essence – it sets up the *not-yet*.

Bloch juxtaposes grey with blue, the colour of hope: 'This blue, as a colour of distance, likewise designates in a graphically symbolic way the future-laden aspect, the Not-Yet-Become in reality.'[34] Goethe defines blue as a 'stimulating nothingness'.[35]

As the upper sky and distant mountains appear blue, so a blue surface seems to retire from us. But as we readily follow an agreeable object that flies from us, so we love to contemplate blue, not because it advances to us, but because it draws us after it.[36]

A society that is without any hope, like today's society, is wrapped in grey. It lacks *distance*.

If we harbour the spirit of hope, we see what is coming even in what is past. What is coming, the truly novel – as the *other* – is a *dream*, the *daydream of the past*. Without the spirit of hope, we are held captive in the same. The spirit of hope seeks out in the past the *traces* of what is coming. In Walter Benjamin's beautiful formulation, the 'past carries with it a temporal index by which it is referred to redemption'.[37]

I am not at all transparent to myself. The conscious sphere within our psyche is very small. It is surrounded by broad dark edges. What is perceived can remain unconscious even though it already determines our actions. Knowledge is located not only in full consciousness but in the semi-conscious. Those insights to which only hope has access have not yet been comprehended. They have not yet become part of consciousness and of what is known. Their mode of being is the 'Not-Yet-Conscious'. They come from the future:

> The Not-Yet-Conscious is thus solely the preconscious of what is to come, the psychological birthplace of the New. And it keeps itself preconscious above all because in fact there is within it a content of consciousness which has not yet become wholly manifest, and is still dawning from the future.[38]

Bloch distinguishes strictly between the Not-Yet-Conscious and the unconscious of psychoanalysis. The psychoanalytic term 'the unconscious' signifies repressed events of the past. *Nothing new* takes place in the space of the unconscious. The unconscious 'is not a newly dawning consciousness with new content but an old one with

old content'.[39] It lacks the *radiance* of what is coming. The unconscious is determined by regression. In it is deposited the uncanny past, which haunts the present and blocks the future. Psychoanalysis may produce insights, but these only illuminate the past. What gains access to the Not-Yet-Conscious, the coming, the not-yet-born, is not regression but progression. The Not-Yet-Conscious is full of positive premonitions, presentiments and colourful reflections. From the unconscious emerge night-dreams. Daydreams, by contrast, are nourished by the Not-Yet-Conscious. The one who hopes, Bloch says, 'scents no musty cellar, but morning air'.[40] The Not-Yet-Conscious is '*the psychological representation of the Not-Yet-Become in an age and its world, on the Front of the world*'.[41] It is a 'phenomenon of the Novum'.[42] Hope plays a major part in bringing about the new.

As mentioned before, hope comes from *somewhere else*. Its *transcendence* links it with *faith*. Bloch, however, deprives it of all *transcendence* by submitting it to the *immanence* of will:

There is never anything soft about conscious-known hope, but a will within it insists: it should be so, it must become so. The wishful and volitional streak vigorously bursts out within it . . . Walking upright is presupposed, a will which refuses to be outvoted by anything that has already become; it has its preserve in this upright posture.[43]

Bloch's hope is robust and rebellious. It does not have a contemplative aspect. However, hope does not stand upright. Walking upright is not its fundamental posture.

It *leans forward in order to listen intensely*. Unlike the will, it does not rebel. Hope is the beat of a wing that *carries* us.

Hope's contemplative aspect means that, for Arendt, hope is inevitably marginalized by the absolute primacy of *vita activa*. Bloch, too, conceives of hope primarily from the perspective of activity. It is inspired by a Promethean will. Bloch casts Job as a *rebel of hope*. In the face of the injustice he has suffered, Job revolts against God. In Bloch's view, Job no longer places his trust in God's righteousness. God is replaced with the 'militant optimism' of the human being:[44] 'it is really in the Book of Job that the great reversal of values begins – the discovery of Utopian potency within the religious sphere: that a man can be better, and behave better, than his God'.[45]

Hope differs fundamentally from Bloch's 'militant optimism'. Amid absolute despair, it *raises* me *up* again. The hopeful become *susceptible* to the new, to the new possibilities that, in the absence of hope, we would not even recognize. The spirit of hope inhabits a field of possibilities that exceeds the immanence of the will. Prognostics make hope superfluous. The hopeful expect the incalculable, *possibilities beyond all likelihood*.

Hope as a Form of Life

Despite being the precise opposite of anxiety, hope struc-
turally resembles it, because – like anxiety but unlike fear,
which always involves a concrete *feared object* – hope is
without an object.[1] Anxiety relates to something altogether
indeterminate. Anxiety concerns being-in-the-world as
such. This indeterminacy is precisely what gives it its
intensity. The object of hope, the *spes qua*, also escapes
any concrete conceptualization. Hope fundamentally
attunes [be-stimmt] our being. Like anxiety, it can therefore be understood as a fundamental *mode of being*, that is,
as an *existential.*

'Mood' is of central importance in Heidegger's *Being
and Time*. The primary 'Da', the sense in which we
are here – 'da' – is not conveyed through an insight or
objective perception but through moods: 'The mood
has already disclosed, in every case, Being-in-the-world

71

as a whole, and makes it possible first of all to direct oneself towards something.'[2] Before we direct our attention at something, *we find ourselves* already in a mood. A mood is not a subjective state that then colours the objects. Rather, it discloses the world at a pre-reflexive level. Even before any conscious perception, we experience the world in a particular mood. On a pre-reflexive level, moods make a '*Da*' accessible. The '*Da*' that is disclosed by a mood *grounds* being-in-the-world and also *attunes* thinking. Being-here is, first of all, being-attuned [Gestimmt-Sein]. We always *find ourselves* already in a mood before we *find something* particular in perception. We are a*lways already* thrown into a mood. The primordial disclosure of being-in-the-world takes place not by way of cognition but by way of a mood.

The predominant fundamental mood in *Being and Time* is anxiety. Heidegger believes that the existential analysis of 'Dasein', his ontological term for the human being, requires the identification of a mood that allows 'the most far-reaching and most primordial possibilities of disclosure' of Dasein's being.[3] According to Heidegger, this mood is anxiety: 'As a state-of-mind which will satisfy these methodological requirements, the phenomenon of anxiety will be made basic for our analysis.'[4] Why is it anxiety that satisfies the 'methodological requirements' of an existential analysis of Dasein? Heidegger's terse answer is that 'in anxiety alone lies the possibility of a distinctive disclosure; for anxiety individualizes'.[5]

Giving ontological priority to anxiety over other moods is, in fact, not merely a 'methodological' decision. It is an *existential* one, because there are moods other than anxiety – positive ones – that disclose and illuminate human existence in much the same way as anxiety. When we feel *joy*, for instance, the world appears very different from the way it appears in negative moods such as anxiety or boredom. By prioritizing anxiety, Heidegger turns individuation, separateness, into an essential trait of human existence. He conceives of human existence primarily from the perspective of being-a-self and not from that of 'being-with'.

According to Heidegger, anxiety arises when the edifice of our familiar daily patterns of perception and behaviour, which we do not usually question, collapses and gives way to a 'not-at-home'.[6] This tears Dasein out of its 'everyday publicness',[7] out of 'the way in which things have been publicly interpreted'.[8] Everydayness interprets the world along conformist lines. Everyone unquestioningly follows the already established forms of apprehending and judging. The 'they' represents this conformist behaviour. It dictates to us how we should act, apprehend, judge, sense and think: 'We take pleasure and enjoy ourselves as *they* [*man*] take pleasure; we read, see, and judge about literature and art as *they* see and judge . . . we find "shocking" what *they* find shocking.'[9] The 'they' alienates Dasein from its potentiality-for-being: 'When Dasein, tranquillized, and "understanding" everything, thus compares itself with everything, it drifts along towards an alienation [Entfremdung] in which its ownmost potentiality-for-Being is hidden from it.'[10] The core argument of *Being and Time* is that it is only when experiencing anxiety that Dasein has disclosed to it the possibility of abandoning the 'they', taking hold of its ownmost self and realizing its ownmost potentiality-for-being. Only the experience of anxiety puts an end to the self's alienated relationship with itself. With anxiety, Dasein finally finds the way to *itself*. 'In uncanniness Dasein stands together with itself primordially.'[11]

By liberating Dasein from the 'everyday publicness of the 'they', in which it lives forgetfully-of-self, anxiety individualizes Dasein and returns it to itself:

> The 'world' can offer nothing more, and neither can the Dasein-with of Others. Anxiety thus takes away from Dasein the possibility of understanding itself, as it falls, in terms of the 'world' and the way things have been publicly interpreted. Anxiety throws Dasein back upon that which it is anxious about – its authentic potentiality-for-Being-in-the-world.[12]

In the experience of anxiety, the familiar 'at-home' slips away from Dasein. The '"at-home" of publicness', the everyday horizon of meaning and understanding, collapses.

Anxiety arises when what grounds the everyday world gives way. In the state of anxiety, a chasm opens. But how can a world be rebuilt on this chasm? How can Dasein act without lapsing back into everydayness? How can Dasein orient itself after the everyday world has collapsed? Where can it find a firm footing? Heidegger obsessively invokes the ownmost self, the ownmost potentiality-for-being, self-constancy [Selbst-ständigkeit]. Is 'resoluteness' in realizing its ownmost self the only way for Dasein 'to "stand" down through the unsecured and unprotected into the abyssal ground'?[13] Is it possible to *stand in the abyss* only if Dasein is resolute in realizing its ownmost self, its self-constancy? Heidegger holds on to the *immanence of the self* and renounces the possibility that Dasein might find a firm footing in something transcendent. Dasein follows nothing but the internal 'call' that asks it to take hold of its ownmost self. For Heidegger, taking hold of one's ownmost self already counts as an action: Dasein 'lets its ownmost Self *take action in itself*'.[14] Taking-action-in-oneself is a pure form of acting, an acting that *pulsates in itself* or *wants itself*, so to speak, without, however, referring to any worldly event.

If the way things were publicly interpreted has collapsed, what criteria does anxious Dasein have to measure its worldly action? Is it now possible for Dasein, standing by itself, to take hold of possibilities of being that differ fundamentally from the 'null' possibilities available to the 'they'?[15] Even in its individualization, Dasein is never entirely free, because it is always already thrown into *specific* possibilities of being. Its 'thrownness' means it cannot freely project possibilities of being. The resoluteness in seeking the ownmost potentiality-for-being does not open up to it the *new*, the *wholly other*: 'In resoluteness the issue for Dasein is its ownmost potentiality-for-Being, which, as something thrown, can project itself only upon *definite factical* possibilities.'[16] In its individualization, Dasein liberates itself from the they's 'null' possibilities of being but at the same time is always already thrown into specific possibilities: 'Dasein, as essentially having a state-of-mind, has already got itself into definite possibilities. . .'.[17] Dasein does not have access to the *unprecedented*, *the coming* possibilities of being. It is incapable of raising itself above *beenness*, the temporality of thrownness. The future, in the sense of 'l'avenir', remains closed to 'anxious' Dasein.[18]

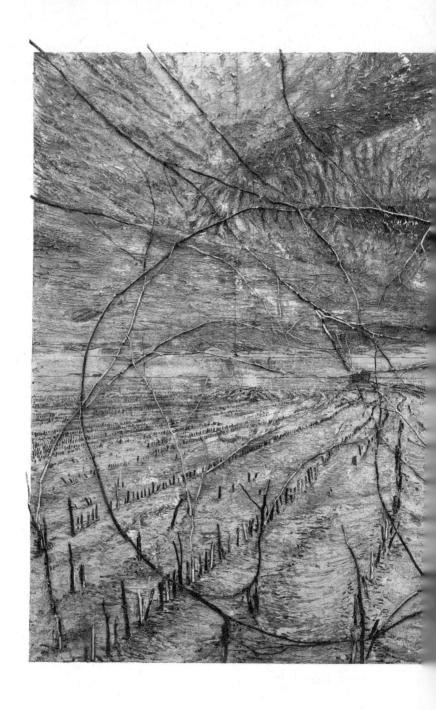

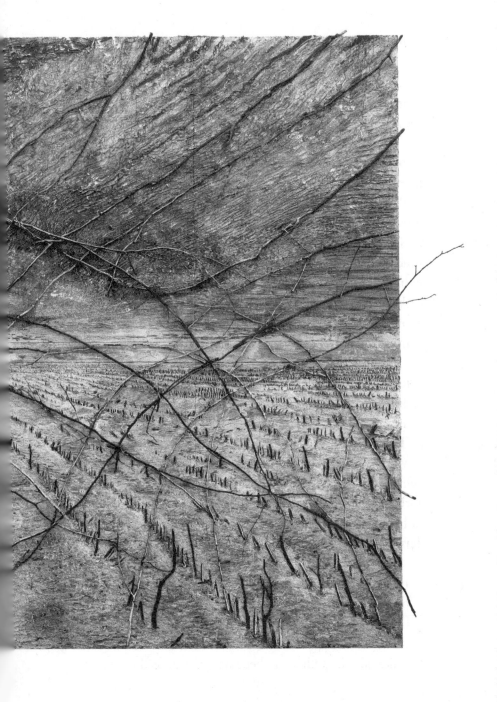

Anxiety radically narrows the *field of possibilities* and thus makes it harder to gain access to the *new*, to the *not-yet-existing*. For this reason, it is opposed to hope, which sharpens the *sense of possibility* and kindles the *passion for the new*, *for the wholly other*. Were we to base our analysis of Dasein on hope rather than anxiety, we would discover a completely different notion of existence, even a *different world*.

Because anxiety tends to isolate Dasein, it does not generate a 'We' that takes the initiative and acts. Heidegger even understands being-with from the perspective of the isolated individual, the perspective of being-oneself. What we might call 'authentic solicitude' – that is, an authentic relation to the other – does not express itself in friendship, love or solidarity. Rather, it must call on the other to take hold of its self in radical individualization. A *community* is not founded on the side-by-side of isolated human beings. Authentic solicitude counteracts *community formation* and reduces *social cohesion*.

The solicitude that lovingly and affectionately turns towards others, that takes care of them – that is, *loving solicitude* – is entirely unknown to Heidegger. As well as authentic solicitude, he describes an inauthentic solicitude, which tries to appropriate the other or to make him dependent:

It can, as it were, take away 'care' from the Other and put itself in his position in concern: it can leap in for him. This kind of solicitude takes over for the Other that with which he is to concern himself. . . . In such solicitude the Other can become one who is dominated and dependent, even if this domination is a tacit one and remains hidden from him.[19]

Solicitude that 'leaps in' for others and 'takes over' their concerns is inauthentic. It makes others 'dependent' and 'dominated'. But who has an interest in appropriating others through solicitude in this way? And even this 'authentic' solicitude, which constantly asks others to seize their ownmost selves rather than become dependent or dominated, seems strange.

According to Heidegger, each self on its own must compensate for the collapse of the institutions that provided *meaning* and *orientation* – the collapse that expresses itself in anxiety. He ignores all forms of existence that transcend the self towards the *other*. Everything circles around the self. In Heidegger's existential analysis of Dasein, there is no place for Gabriel Marcel's formula of hope: 'I hope in thee for us.'

Hope does not receive its energy from the immanence of the self. It does not have its centre in the self. Rather, the hopeful are on their way towards the *other*. In hope, one places *one's trust* in what *exceeds* the self. Hope therefore approximates *faith*. It is the *authority of the other* as a *transcendence* that raises me up in the face of absolute despair, that enables me *to stand in the abyss*. The hopeful do not owe their *standing* to *themselves*. That is why Havel believes that hope originates in the transcendent – that it comes *from the distance*.

What is specific to moods, as opposed to feelings or affects, is that they intend *nothing in particular*. The hopeful need not have a *concrete goal*. A wish or expectation, by contrast, remains attached to a concrete matter. Thus it is possible for a human being merely to hope. Someone who merely expects or merely wishes is an absurdity: expecting and wishing are not moods; that is, they do not represent *modes of being*.

Ernst Bloch conceives of hope as an affect. At the same time, he disputes Heidegger's notion of 'mood' because he denies it the disclosing character that distinguishes it from an affect. A mood discloses *Being* by *attuning* [be-*stimmen*] being-in-the-world. Unlike a mood, an affect does not seize being-in-the-world. Moods precede any perception of objects by *grounding* them.

Bloch takes a 'thereabouts' as the fundamental character of moods:

> It is an essential feature of the mood that it appears total only when it is diffuse; it never consists of a dominant, overwhelming emotion [Affekt], but of an itself wide mixture of many emotional feelings [Affektgefühle] which have not yet been settled. This in fact makes it into a phenomenon which so easily becomes iridescent, this at the same time causes it – still on the other side of the confusion of sounds before the beginning of a piece of music, and also completely without intensive density – to spin out and deform so easily as merely impressionistic experience-reality (Debussy, Jacobsen). Heidegger also hails from this impressionistic thereabouts, in so far as he describes it and at the same time succumbs to it. . . . But Heidegger has not got beyond the dull, depressingly stagnant, even shallow dimension that he has uncovered.[20]

The intentionality of moods is entirely different from that of affects. A mood seems 'diffuse' because it does not address an object, a counterpart. Its objectless intention, which *attunes* every perception in advance, makes it appear 'diffuse'. In fact, it is always fully *attuned*.[21] Contrary to Bloch's assumption, moods do not dissolve form; they provide it. As *fundamental moods*, they represent the fundamental form of being-in-the-world. A mood is far from an 'impressionistic experience-reality'. In fact, it precedes experience. Experiences come *after* mood. Bloch fails to recognize mood's *precedence*.

A mood *opens up* the world *as such, before anything specific* appears. It inhabits the *pro-scenium* of perception. Moods are this side of affects, *preceding* them. Thus they are more *attuning* and more *attuned* than any 'dominant, overwhelming emotion'. They *dominate* without ruling, without overpowering. This gives them an *ontological priority* over affects.

As a *fundamental mood*, hope is not tied to a worldly event. Hope is independent of how things will end. If hope is taken to be an affect, its specific character as a mood and its *gravity*, which suffuses all of Dasein, are lost. Unlike hope, expectations and wishes are bound up with an object or a worldly event. Hope is *open*, and moves into the *open*.

Faith also has two different types of intentionality. Faith as *fides qua creditor* – the faith that believes – is a *fundamental attitude*. Thus we can meaningfully speak of a believer. As a fundamental attitude, this faith is not bound up with any concrete article of faith. By contrast, faith as *fides quae creditor* – the faith in which someone believes – concerns articles of faith.

As opposed to *spes quae* (hoping that), hope as *spes qua* (hoping) stands above worldly events. As a *spiritual state*, it owes its intensity, its depth, to the absence of an intentional object. Thus Gabriel Marcel remarks that 'hope, by a *nisus* [effort] which is peculiar to it, tends inevitably to transcend the particular objects to which it at first seems to be attached'.[22]

Because of its 'thrownness', Heidegger's Dasein is not the *master of its being*. It cannot seize its being. Its freedom is limited by its thrownness: 'As being, Dasein is something that has been thrown; it has been brought into its "there", but not of its own accord.'[23] Dasein's thrownness is characterized by the fact that Dasein has *not* itself laid the ground of its being: 'This "not" belongs to the existential meaning of "thrownness".'[24] Thrownness expresses itself as a *burden* or *heaviness*. For Heidegger, even elated moods reveal the character of existence as a burden: 'Furthermore, a mood of elation can alleviate the manifest burden of Being; that such a mood is possible also discloses the burdensome character of Dasein, even while it alleviates the burden.'[25] Dasein cannot throw off its existential burden. Nothing liberates it from its burdensome character.

Being and Time fails to complement 'everydayness' with a concept of festiveness. Outside of 'everydayness', there is only *anxiety*. Festiveness is the exact opposite of 'everydayness'. Heidegger's Dasein is ceaselessly *working*. Its world, its environment, is ultimately a workshop. Festivities, the *other of work*, are unknown to it. The festive feeling is a mood, a mood of elation, in which even 'care', which Heidegger takes to be an essential trait of Dasein, is suspended. During a *festivity*, the human being is *without care*.

One passage of *Being and Time* contains a brief discussion of hope:

Hope has sometimes been characterized as the expectation of a *bonum futurum*, to distinguish it from fear, which relates itself to a *malum futurum*. But what is decisive for the structure of hope as a phenomenon, is not so much the 'futural' character of that *to which* it relates itself but rather the existential meaning of *hoping itself*. Even here its character as a mood lies primarily in hoping as *hoping for something for oneself* [Für-sich-erhoffen]. He who hopes takes himself *with* him into his hope, as it were, and brings himself up against what he hopes for. But this presupposes that he has somehow arrived at himself. To say that hope *brings alleviation* [erleichtert] from depressing misgivings, means merely that even hope, as a state-of-mind, is still related to our burdens, and related in the mode of *Being*-as-having been.[26]

In this passage, Heidegger distorts the phenomenon of hope in order to force it into the architecture of his existential analysis of Dasein. First, it is reduced to 'hoping for something for oneself'. But hope does not circle around the self. Its fundamental character is not that of one's having 'arrived at oneself'. Rather, the hopeful move *beyond themselves*. The fundamental formula of hope is 'to rely on'.[27] Gabriel Marcel's phrase, 'I hope in thee for us', brings out the aspect of hope that transcends the self towards a *We*.

Hope, faith and love are related. Achim von Arnim calls them the 'the three sisters fair'.[28] All three are turned towards the *other*. Those who hope, love or believe devote *themselves* to the *other*; they transcend the immanence of the self. But neither love nor faith has a place in

83

Heidegger's thinking, which lacks the aspect of the *other*. Those who cannot move beyond themselves can neither love nor hope.

Heidegger's Dasein is either a slave to the 'everyday' or 'anxious about the potentiality-for-Being'.[29] Elated moods or high spirits do not belong to its essence. Heidegger holds fast to Dasein's burdensome character. Even hope is derived from it. But in fact, hope, as an elated mood, lifts us out of the burden of existence. Hope *unburdens* and relieves Dasein. It enables us to leap across a gulf; it is a spring that elevates us above 'thrownness' and 'guilt'. Heidegger's Dasein is *inexcusable* [*unentschuld-bar*]. Mercy is impossible. Hope, however, is receptive to *mercy*. Heidegger also misjudges the temporality of hope, conceiving it from the perspective of the 'mode of *Being*-as-having been'.[30] Hope, however, is characterized by the mode of not-yet-being. The *future in the sense of 'l'avenir'* remains closed to Heidegger.

Hope makes us receptive to possibilities into which we are not *thrown* but rather *dream* ourselves. Heidegger's Dasein does not dream into the future. It is incapable of daydreaming. Instead, it is haunted by anxiety dreams and nightmares. Anxiety has no access to the future as a space of possibilities. It is neither anticipatory nor visionary. Hope, by contrast, discloses futurity to us: what is coming, the not-yet-born, the latent, the becoming. It is a *messianic mood*.

Heidegger's thinking is Greek to the extent that it is oriented towards *beenness* [*Gewesenes*], towards *essence* [*Wesen*]. He therefore defines even the possible [*das Mögliche*] from the perspective of *essence*. Heidegger's possible is not what is coming, the unprecedented; rather, as the 'may be' [das Mög-liche],[31] as what is worth being favoured [*das Mögenswerte*], it signifies the release of a thing or person into their 'essence' – 'the bestowal of their essence as a gift'.[32] Heidegger also conceives of 'enabling' [Vermögen] from the perspective of favouring [Mögen]:

> Man can think in the sense that he possesses the possibility to do so. This possibility [das Mögliche] alone, however, is no guarantee to us that we are capable of thinking [es vermögen]. For we are capable only of what we favour, what we are inclined to do by way of letting it be. And again, we truly incline only toward something that already favours us, and favours us in our essential being by inclining toward it.[33]

In Heidegger, essence [Wesen], beenness [das Gewesene], is always at the centre. There is no opening that points beyond the closed nature of essence. Things must be captured or preserved in their essence, that is, in their beenness. It is essence as beenness that we approach by favouring it, *not in a movement ahead but in a backwards movement – not by dreaming but by remembering*. The concern is always preserving, not *daring*. Heidegger's thinking is guided by Mnemosyne, not Elpis. Being is having-been that must be wrested from an obstinate oblivion. Truth as 'unconcealment' works its way out of oblivion, 'the concealing of the as yet unrevealed essence'.[34] Heidegger's thinking is caught between forgetting and remembering. As a result, it has no access to the coming, that is, to the *future as 'l'avenir'*.

Heidegger's thinking has no sense for the *possible*, for a *coming* that transcends the 'favouring' and 'enabling'

85

in which *essence* expresses itself. His thinking is closed to the *radically new*, the *wholly other*. It is 'on the way' to *what has been*, to *essence*. Anxiety is ultimately the fear of death. Heidegger's thinking is attuned [be-*stimmt*] not by *birth* but by *death*. This focus on death blinds Heidegger's thought to what-is-not-yet, to the *unborn*. The *thinking of hope* takes as its point of orientation not death but birth – not 'being-in-the-world' but *coming-into-the-world*. *Hope hopes beyond death*. The characteristic movement of thinking that hopes is not 'anticipation of death' but *anticipation of a new birth*. The fundamental formula of hope is the *coming-into-the-world of birth*.

Notes

Prelude

1 Barack Obama, 'Farewell Address', delivered 10 January 2017; available at https://obamawhitehouse.archives.gov /farewell.

2 Friedrich Kluge, *Etymologisches Wörterbuch der deutschen Sprache*, Berlin: De Gruyter, 1986, p. 313.

3 KJV, Romans 5:3–5.

4 Friedrich Nietzsche, *Nachgelassene Fragmente 1875–1879*, in *Kritische Studienausgabe*, vol. 8, Berlin and New York: De Gruyter 1988, p. 445.

5 Terry Eagleton, *Hope Without Optimism*, New Haven: Yale University Press, 2015, p. 3.

6 Gabriel Marcel, *Homo Viator: Introduction to a Metaphysic of Hope*, Chicago: Henry Regnery Company, 1951, p. 53; emphasis added.

7 Ernst Bloch, *The Principle of Hope*, vol. 1, Cambridge, MA: MIT Press, 1996, p. 147.

8 KJV, Romans 8:24.

9 Marcel, *Homo Viator*, p. 52.

10 *Derrida*, documentary by Amy Ziering and Kirby Dick, 2002; available at https://www.youtube.com/watch?v=FF IKZZD7By4. The relevant passage at 00:29–01:40.

11 Simone Weil, quoted after Simone Pétremont, *Simone Weil: A Life*, New York: Pantheon Books, 1976, p. 340.

12 Georg Wilhelm Friedrich Hegel, *Lectures on the History of Philosophy*, vol. 3, London: Kegan Paul, Trench, Trübner, 1895, pp. 546f.; transl. modified.

13 Walter Benjamin, 'Experience and Poverty', in *Selected Writings*, vol. 2, part 2 (1931–1934), Cambridge, MA: Harvard University Press, 1999, pp. 731–6; here: pp. 732f.

14 Marcel, *Homo Viator*, p. 60.

15 Ibid., p. 44.

16 Bloch, *The Principle of Hope*, vol. 1, p. 3.

17 Transl. note: Bloch actually makes a similar point. Without the omission, the sentence quoted above runs: 'But now *that the creators of fear have been dealt with*, a feeling that suits us better is overdue'; emphasis added.

18 Gabriel Marcel, *The Mystery of Being*, vol. 2: *Faith and Reality*, Chicago: Henry Regnery Company, 1951, p. 160.

19 Mark Fisher, *Capitalist Realism: Is There No Alternative?* Winchester: Zero Books, 2009, p. 3.

Hope and Acting

1 Albert Camus, *The Myth of Sisyphus*, London: Penguin, 1955, p. 3.

2 Albert Camus, 'Summer in Algiers', in *Lyrical and Critical Essays*, New York: Vintage Books, 1970, pp. 80–92; here: pp. 91f.

3 Friedrich Nietzsche, *Human, All Too Human*, Cambridge: Cambridge University Press, p. 45; transl. modified. Transl. note: The omitted end of the last sentence puts

a different slant on this: 'To that end he gives men hope: it is in truth the worst of all evils, because it protracts the torment of men.'

4 Albert Camus, 'The World Moves Quickly', in *Camus at Combat: Writing 1944–1947*, Princeton, NJ: Princeton University Press, 2006, pp. 268–70; here: p. 270.

5 Camus, *The Myth of Sisyphus*, p. 29.

6 Ibid. Transl. note: The German edition has 'Sehnsucht' ('longing') instead of 'nostalgia'. The French original is 'La pensée d'un homme est avant tout sa nostalgie.' Albert Camus, *Le Mythe de Sisyphe*, Anjou, Quebec: Éditions CEC, 2012, p. 80.

7 Camus, *The Myth of Sisyphus*, p. 71. *Le Mythe de Sisyphe*, p. 127.

8 Albert Camus, 'The Enigma', in *Lyrical and Critical Essays*, pp. 154–61, here: p. 160.

9 Albert Camus, 'Create Dangerously', in *Committed Writings*, New York: Vintage, 2020, pp. 105–33; here: p. 133.

10 Benedict de Spinoza, *Ethics Preceded by On the Improvement of the Understanding*, New York: Hafner, 1954, p. 223.

11 Ibid., p. 224.

12 Bloch, *The Principle of Hope*, vol. 1, p. 112.

13 Transl. note: 'Mood' (*Stimmung*) is a Heideggerian term: 'Mood is the fundamental way in which Dasein is open to itself and its world.' Entry on 'Mood' in Mark A. Wrathall (ed.), *The Cambridge Heidegger Lexicon*, Cambridge: Cambridge University Press, 2021, p. 500.

14 Eagleton, *Hope Without Optimism*, pp. 56f.

15 Transl. note: In the context of Heidegger, 'Angst' is translated as 'anxiety', and 'Furcht' as 'fear'. See the entry on these terms in *The Cambridge Heidegger Lexicon*, pp. 37–9.

16 Ludwig Wittgenstein, *Philosophical Investigations*, 4th

ed., Chichester: Wiley-Blackwell, 2009, 'Philosophy of Psychology' (formerly Part II of *Philosophical Investigations*), section I, §1, p. 183e.

17 Erich Fromm, *The Revolution of Hope: Toward A Humanized Technology*, New York: Bantam Books, 1968, p. 9.

18 Ibid., p. 12.

19 Friedrich Nietzsche, *Daybreak*, Cambridge: Cambridge University Press, 1997, p. 223.

20 Ibid.

21 Martin Luther King, 'I Have a Dream', quoted after the official transcript at The National Archives and Records Administration, available at: https://www.archives.gov/files/social-media/transcripts/transcript-march-pt3-of-3-2602934.pdf.

22 Bloch, *The Principle of Hope*, vol. 1, p. 159.

23 See Sigmund Freud, *Introductory Lectures on Psychoanalysis*, London: Penguin, 1991, p. 420: 'We know that such day-dreams are the nucleus and prototype of night-dreams. A night-dream is at bottom nothing other than a daydream that has been made utilizable owing to the liberation of the instinctual impulses at night, and that has been distorted by the form assumed by mental activity at night.'

24 Bloch, *The Principle of Hope*, vol. 1, pp. 91f.

25 Hannah Arendt, *The Human Condition*, Chicago: University of Chicago Press, 1998 [1958], p. 247.

26 Ibid., p. 233.

27 Ibid., p. 238.

28 Ibid., p. 240.

29 Ibid., p. 244.

30 Ibid., p. 245.

31 Hannah Arendt, *Vita Activa oder Vom tätigen Leben*, Munich: Piper, 1981, p. 241. Transl. note: The quotation within the quotation (absent in the English edition of Arendt's text) is from Friedrich Nietzsche, *On the*

Genealogy of Morality, Cambridge: Cambridge University Press, 2007, p. 37.
32 Arendt, *The Human Condition*, p. 246.
33 Ibid.
34 Ibid.
35 Ibid., pp. 246f.
36 Ibid., p. 247.
37 Johann Sebastian Bach, *Christmas Oratorio*, part 1.
38 Arendt, *The Human Condition*, p. 245. Transl. note: There is a subtle difference between the English and German editions. The English has: 'The force that keeps them [people acting in concert] together, as distinguished from the space of appearances in which they gather and the power which keeps this public space in existence, is the force of mutual promise or contract' (pp. 244f.). The German says: 'Die Kraft, die diese Versammelten zusammenhält, . . . ist die bindende Kraft gegenseitiger Versprechen, die sich schließlich in dem Vertrag niederschlägt' (*Vita Activa*, p. 240): 'The force that keeps those assembled together . . . is the binding force of mutual promises which finally is translated into the form of the contract.'
39 Jürgen Moltmann, *Theology of Hope: On the Ground and the Implications of a Christian Theology*, New York: Harper & Row, 1967, pp. 33f.
40 Ibid., p. 35.
41 Ibid., p. 19.
42 Ibid., p. 35.
43 Paul Celan, 'Speech on the Occasion of Receiving the Literature Prize of the Free Hanseatic City of Bremen', in *Collected Prose*, Manchester: Carcanet, 1986, pp. 33–5; here: p. 34; transl. modified. Transl. note: The English version translates 'unverloren' – literally 'not lost' or 'not forlorn' – as 'secure'. I substituted 'not forlorn' to bring out the associations followed by the argument.

44 Ingeborg Bachmann, *Ein Tag wird kommen: Gespräche in Rom: Ein Porträt von Gerda Haller*, Salzburg: Jung und Jung, 2004, p. 55; emphasis B.-C. Han.

45 Ibid., pp. 79ff., emphasis B.-C. Han.

46 Ingeborg Bachmann, *In the Storm of Roses: Selected Poems*, Princeton: Princeton University Press, 1986, p. 177.

47 Franz Kafka, fragment from 'The Eight Octavo Note-Books', in *Wedding Preparations in the Country and other Posthumous Prose Writings*, London: Secker & Warburg, 1954, p. 132.

48 KJV, Romans 4:18.

49 Franz Kafka, 'The Great Wall of China', in *The Complete Stories*, New York: Schocken Books, 1988, pp. 235–48; here: p. 244.

50 Ibid., p. 237.

51 Ibid., p. 244.

52 Ibid., p. 241.

53 Ibid., pp. 237f.

54 Václav Havel, *Disturbing the Peace: A Conversation with Karel Hvížd'ala*, New York: Vintage, 1991, p. 181.

55 Walter Benjamin, 'Hashish in Marseille', in *Selected Writings*, vol. 2, part 2 (1931–1934), Cambridge, MA: Harvard University Press, pp. 673–9; here: p. 678.

56 Paul Celan, 'Thread Suns', in *Selected Poems*, London: Penguin, 1995, p. 235.

57 Martin Heidegger, *Being and Time*, Oxford: Blackwell, 1962, p. 417.

58 Transl. note: It is worth keeping in mind that Heidegger also used 'Wesen' as a verb – 'essencing', 'bringing about' – indicating an active aspect of being as something expressing itself through its effects.

59 Bloch, *The Principle of Hope*, vol. 1, p. 112.

60 Ibid., p. 198.

61 Ibid., p. 336.

62 Eagleton, *Hope Without Optimism*, p. 100.

63 Ibid., p. 110.

64 Ernst Bloch, 'Can Hope Be Disappointed?', in *Literary Essays*, Stanford: Stanford University Press, 1998, pp. 339–45; here: pp. 340f.

65 Claudio Monteverdi, *Orfeo: Favola in Musica/Orfeo: A Tale in Music*, beginning of Act III, quoted after Boston Early Music Festival, Chamber Opera Series 2012, p. 10; available at: https://web.archive.org/web/20130705013834/http://www.bemf.org/media/1213_opera_libretto.pdf.

Hope and Knowledge

1 www2.univ-paris8.fr/deleuze/article.php3?id_article =131. See also Philippe Mengue, *Faire l'idiot: La politique de Deleuze*, Paris: Editions Germina, 2013. Transl. note: The concept of 'idiot' is also explained in Gilles Deleuze and Félix Guattari, *What is Philosophy?*, New York: Columbia University Press, 1994, pp. 61–70.

2 Max Scheler, 'Love and Knowledge', in *On Feeling, Knowing, and Valuing*, Chicago: University of Chicago Press, 1992, pp. 147–65; here: p. 147.

3 Ibid.

4 Ibid.

5 Saint Augustine, quoted in Moltmann, *Theology of Hope*, p. 36.

6 Scheler, 'Love and Knowledge', p. 164.

7 Martin Heidegger, Letter of 14 February 1950, in *Letters to His Wife* (1915–1970), Cambridge: Polity, 2008, p. 123.

8 Deleuze and Guattari, *What is Philosophy?*, p. 3.

9 Ibid., pp. 3f.

10 Georg Wilhelm Friedrich Hegel, *The Science of Logic*, vol. 1 (book 2), Cambridge: Cambridge University Press, 2010, p. 337.

11 Transl. note: See *The Cambridge Heidegger Lexicon*, p. 140

(note 7): 'Heidegger concocts the neologism "beenness" (Gewesenheit) to name the distinctive way in which Dasein has a past, and he takes over the Husserlian term "enpresenting" (Gegenwärtigen) to name Dasein's distinctive present.' The term 'Gewesenheit' has also been translated as 'having been' (Heidegger, *Being and Time*, p. 373), or 'having-been-ness' (*The Cambridge Heidegger Lexicon*, p. 269).

12 Martin Heidegger, *The Essence of Truth: On Plato's Cave Allegory and Theaetetus*, London: Continuum, 2002, p. 170.

13 Martin Heidegger, *Contributions to Philosophy (Of the Event)*, Bloomington: Indiana University Press, 2012, p. 113.

14 Ibid., p. 329.

15 Moltmann, *Theology of Hope*, p. 35; emphasis added.

16 Ibid., p. 33.

17 Ibid., p. 20.

18 Quoted after ibid., p. 35.

19 Friedrich Nietzsche, *Unpublished Fragments from the Period of Thus Spoke Zarathustra (Summer 1882–Winter 1883/84)*, Stanford: Stanford University Press, 2019, p. 545.

20 Moltmann, *Theology of Hope*, p. 36.

21 Georg Wilhelm Friedrich Hegel, *Elements of the Philosophy of Right*, Cambridge: Cambridge University Press, 1991, p. 23.

22 Carl Ludwig Michelet, *Wahrheit aus meinem Leben*, Berlin: Nicolai'sche Verlagsbuchhandlung, 1884, p. 90.

23 Walter Benjamin, *The Arcades Project*, Cambridge, MA: Harvard University Press, 1999, p. 389.

24 Ibid., p. 388.

25 Ibid., p. 863.

26 Ibid., p. 827.

27 Marcel Proust, *In Search of Lost Time, Vol VI: Time Regained*, London: Vintage, 1996, p. 246.

28 Marcel Proust, *In Search of Lost Time, Vol. V: The Captive*, New York: The Modern Library, 1993, p. 456.

29 Theodor Adorno, *Minima Moralia: Reflections on a Damaged Life*, London: Verso, 2005, p. 98.

30 Ibid., p. 222.

31 Theodor Adorno, 'Perennial Fashion: On Jazz', in *Prisms*, Cambridge, MA: MIT Press, 1997, pp. 119–32; here: p. 132.

32 Adorno, *Minima Moralia*, pp. 224f.

33 Ernst Bloch, *Philosophische Grundfragen I: Zur Ontologie des Noch-Nicht-Seins*, Frankfurt am Main: Suhrkamp, 1961, p. 23.

34 Bloch, *The Principle of Hope*, vol. 1, p. 127.

35 Johann Wolfgang Goethe, *Theory of Colours*, London: John Murray, 1840, §779, p. 311; transl. modified.

36 Ibid., §§780f., p. 311.

37 Walter Benjamin, 'Theses on the Philosophy of History', in *Illuminations: Essays and Reflections*, New York: Schocken, 2007, pp. 253–64; here: p. 254.

38 Bloch, *The Principle of Hope*, vol. 1, p. 116.

39 Ibid., p. 115.

40 Ibid., p. 116.

41 Ibid., p. 127.

42 Ibid.

43 Ibid., p. 147

44 Ernst Bloch, *Atheism in Christianity: The Religion of the Exodus and the Kingdom*, London: Verso, 2009, p. 231.

45 Ibid., p. 94.

Hope as a Form of Life

1 Translator's note: In this chapter 'anxiety' translates 'Angst' and 'fear' translates 'Furcht'. In previous passages,

unless they explicitly engage with Heidegger, 'Angst' has been translated as 'fear' whenever this seemed more natural.

2 Heidegger, *Being and Time*, p. 176.
3 Ibid., p. 226.
4 Ibid., p. 227.
5 Ibid., p. 235; transl. amended.
6 Ibid., p. 233.
7 Ibid.
8 Ibid., p. 235.
9 Ibid., p. 164.
10 Ibid., p. 222.
11 Ibid., p. 333.
12 Ibid., p. 232.
13 Heidegger, *Contributions to Philosophy (Of the Event)*, pp. 383f.
14 Heidegger, *Being and Time*, p. 334.
15 Ibid. Transl. note: Heidegger's 'Nichtigkeit' and 'nichtig' are usually translated as 'nullity' and 'null' (as in 'null and void', German: 'null und nichtig'). Thus, 'auf dem nichtigen Grunde seines nichtigen Entwerfens', the passage from which Han quotes, becomes 'the null basis of its [Dasein's] null projection'.
16 Ibid., p. 346; emphasis B.-C. Han.
17 Ibid., p. 183.
18 Ibid., p. 322.
19 Ibid., p. 158.
20 Bloch, *The Principle of Hope*, vol. 1, p. 105.
21 Transl. note: The German here is again 'be-*stimmt*', which outside Heidegger's terminology would be 'determined', hence the opposite of 'diffuse'.
22 Marcel, *Homo Viator*, p. 32.
23 Heidegger, *Being and Time*, p. 329.
24 Ibid., p. 330.

25 Ibid., p. 173.

26 Ibid., pp. 395–6.

27 Transl. note: The German for 'to rely on' is '*Sich-verlassen-auf*'. The italics hint at hope involving a trust that allows one to leave oneself behind and rely on something or someone outside oneself.

28 Achim von Arnim and Clemens Brentano, *Des Knaben Wunderhorn: Alte deutsche Lieder*, Frankfurt am Main: Insel, 2011, p. 132.

29 Heidegger, *Being and Time*, p. 310.

30 Ibid., p. 396.

31 Martin Heidegger, 'Letter on Humanism', in *Pathmarks*, Cambridge: Cambridge University Press, 1998, pp. 239–76; here: p. 242.

32 Ibid., p. 241.

33 Martin Heidegger, *What is Called Thinking?*, New York: Harper & Row, 1968, p. 3. Transl. note: Han quotes from a talk that Heidegger delivered on the Bavarian broadcasting station in 1952, and which is included in volume 7 of his *Gesammelte Werke*. The talk was based on the first of the lectures that made up the eponymous lecture course at Freiburg in 1951–52 but deviates significantly by both omitting and adding material. The translation has been amended in line with these changes.

34 Martin Heidegger, 'On the Question of Being', in *Pathmarks*, pp. 291–322; here: p. 314.